T0356160

THOMAS JEFFERSON

and the

KENTUCKY CONSTITUTION

THOMAS JEFFERSON

—— *and the* ——

KENTUCKY CONSTITUTION

DENIS FLEMING JR.

Foreword by Sheryl G. Snyder

THE
History
PRESS

Published by The History Press
Charleston, SC
www.historypress.com

Copyright © 2025 by Denis Fleming Jr.

All rights reserved

Frontispiece: Bust of Thomas Jefferson from life by Jean-Antoine Houdon, Paris, 1789. *Library of Congress, photo credit Bruce Greenstein.*

First published 2025

Manufactured in the United States

ISBN 9781467158282

Library of Congress Control Number: 2024947395

Notice: The information in this book is true and complete to the best of our knowledge. It is offered without guarantee on the part of the author or The History Press. The author and The History Press disclaim all liability in connection with the use of this book.

All rights reserved. No part of this book may be reproduced or transmitted in any form whatsoever without prior written permission from the publisher except in the case of brief quotations embodied in critical articles and reviews.

When Mr. Jefferson returned from France, the federal constitution had been adopted; and…he obtained permission to go to Monticello for some months. John Breckinridge and George Nicholas paid him a visit there and informed him that Kentucky was about to frame a constitution for herself, and that Virginia was about to permit Kentucky to become a separate and independent state. He told them there was danger in the federal constitution because the clause defining the powers of the departments of government was not sufficiently guarded and that the first thing to be provided for by the Kentucky constitution should be to confine the judiciary to its powers and the legislative and executive to theirs. Mr. Jefferson drew the form of the provision and gave it to Nicholas and Breckinridge; And it was taken by Nicholas to the convention which met at Danville and there presented it—Breckinridge not being present at the convention. There was much discussion and dissent when the article was offered, but, when its author was made known, the respect of Kentucky for the great name of Jefferson carried it through and it was at once adopted.

—Justice George DuRelle of the Kentucky Supreme Court
(then called the Kentucky Court of Appeals), dissenting in the Court's decision
Commissioners of Sinking Fund v. George *(1898)*

CONTENTS

FOREWORD

Denis Fleming Jr. is a well-known and well-respected Kentucky lawyer with an illustrious career in public service spanning decades. With the publication of this book, he can add "constitutional scholar" to his credentials. The book is impeccably researched history and some part personal memoir. Together, it is a "good read," as the saying goes.

Much has been written about the separation of governmental powers under the Constitution of Kentucky (including my 1984 *Kentucky Law Journal* article), but this book accesses historical resources rarely if ever used on this topic. Specifically, Denis located the papers of George Nicholas—the principal author of the first Constitution of Kentucky—in the Reuben Durrett Collection of George Nicholas Papers at the Hanna Holborn Gray Special Collections Research Center, University of Chicago Library. The Nicholas Papers demonstrate the influence of Thomas Jefferson on the drafting of Kentucky's unusually forceful separation of powers clauses. And Jefferson's role has been a matter of debate in the opinions of Kentucky's appellate courts.

In 1898, a justice of what is now the Kentucky Supreme Court asserted that Nicholas and John Breckinridge met with Jefferson at Monticello and that Jefferson gave them the draft clauses, which Nicholas introduced at the 1792 Kentucky Constitutional Convention, specifically attributing the drafting to Jefferson. One subsequent Kentucky Supreme Court justice questioned that account because it did not cite any supporting evidence. Recently, a judge of the Court of Appeals called the account a "hoax."[1]

But Fleming found in the George Nicholas Papers, including drafts of his speeches to the convention, direct attribution of the separation of powers clauses to the writings of Jefferson. Why is this important? After all, many well-trained lawyers in that era were well versed in Montesquieu's separation of powers analysis. John Adams had authored a specific separation of powers clause in the first Constitution of Massachusetts in 1779. The answer is twofold.

First, at the time of Kentucky's first constitutional convention, it was part of Virginia—and long had been. And there was no more revered Virginia statesman than Thomas Jefferson. By announcing to the convention Jefferson's "authorship" of the separation of powers clauses, Nicholas was invoking a totemic imprimatur. Even if "authorship" was an embellishment, Fleming demonstrates that Jefferson's writings directly influenced the wording of the clauses.

Second, the Kentucky separation of powers clauses are (in the words of the Kentucky Supreme Court) "unusually forceful." In addition to the vesting clauses that vest the governmental power in the three branches of government, the separation of powers clauses are (again in the words of the Kentucky Supreme Court) "double barreled." Section 27 provides that the legislative, executive and judicial power shall each be vested in a distinct branch of government. That is not an uncommon provision in a state constitution. It is the one-sentence clause John Adams included in the Massachusetts Constitution.

But the Kentucky Constitution has a second clause (Section 28) that prohibits any person or group of persons in one branch from exercising any power properly belonging to another branch. This is the clause that has been decisive in many separation of powers cases in Kentucky. And Fleming's research demonstrates that this provision was derived from the ideas and writings of Jefferson.

So, Fleming's book is a work of original research that makes an important contribution to Kentucky history and constitutional law.

—SHERYL G. SNYDER

Mr. Snyder is a member of the University of Kentucky J. David Rosenberg College of Law Hall of Fame and a Fellow in the American Academy of Appellate Lawyers. He is coauthor of The Separation of Governmental Powers Under the Constitution of Kentucky, *a Legal and Historical Analysis of* LRC v. Brown, 664 S.W.2d 907 (Ky. 1984).

INTRODUCTION

Political and policy campaigns, much like military ones, are rich with examples of lost opportunities and hotly debated decisions that produced outcomes by the barest of margins. Similarly, the making of public policy in Kentucky is a product of not so much what we see on cable news or online but a complex web of personal relations, tradeoffs and deal-making that never makes the light of day. What I endeavor to do in this book, from twenty-five years in positions of responsibility in state and federal government, is reveal the hidden dynamics behind some of the most important policy decisions in Kentucky's history and the critical role the state's constitution played in them.

If I ever spent much time considering Kentucky's constitution prior to my tenure in state government, I certainly don't remember it. But I learned quickly how very much alive this over two-hundred-year-old document remains and the essential role it played in the great advances in public policy in Kentucky history. Critical reforms in the creation of jobs, in education and the structure of government itself have been bound up in interpretations of our constitution by Kentucky's courts, by our governors and by elected representatives in the General Assembly. The tension between Kentucky's three branches of government and the direction in the state constitution to these branches to respect one another's power, in wording influenced by Thomas Jefferson himself, has played a central role in the progress of Kentucky.

Many may never have heard of the separation of powers provisions favored by Jefferson and placed in Kentucky's constitution in the 1790s, provisions that enshrine the unusual independence of each branch of the state's government. These provisions are not found in our federal Constitution. This inspiration from Jefferson in the state constitution was apparently a product of the very type of factionalism that we see today in state and national politics.

Moreover, this book details the secret history of the "Kentucky Resolutions" prepared by Jefferson and adopted by the General Assembly in 1798 and 1799 but which failed to get traction among other states except Virginia. These Resolutions, introduced by young Kentucky state representative John Breckinridge, said that Kentucky has the right to declare as unconstitutional and nullify any law enacted by the federal Congress and has unsettling lessons for our current political climate.

Jefferson's secret authorship of these Resolutions, and their use as vehicles for his frustration with President John Adams and the Alien and Sedition Acts, makes for compelling history. As a new state of immigrants, there were protests across Kentucky in opposition to these acts, which criminalized criticism of the national government and directed the arrest and deportation of foreign-born Americans. Jefferson and Kentucky's opposition to these laws, which has meaning in our current political climate, was close in time to Jefferson's guidance on Kentucky's constitution. It was this work, in conjunction with John Breckinridge and George Nicholas, that left Kentucky a legacy of progress.

Admittedly ambitious, this book relates fresh perspectives and new sources validating the influence of Jefferson on Kentucky's constitution and the role of this charter in the great policy decisions of our time—decisions made by Kentucky's courts with Jefferson's legacy in mind and political decisions made under stress where tradeoffs and strong personalities often prevailed. And along the way, this book relates personal profiles and unique experiences of current and past political leaders.

These include figures such as Jefferson; John Adams; Henry Clay; the state's first governor, Isaac Shelby; James Madison; and the little-known but influential John Breckinridge. Four governors of Kentucky, state attorneys general and justices of Kentucky's Supreme Court, including Chief Justice Robert Stephens, who penned many of these court decisions, are also profiled with behind-the-scenes stories. These perspectives are informed by the rich history of Kentucky's constitution, the very dynamics of which are alive today.

In the choice of sources for this book, I used historical records; firsthand accounts; the correspondences of Jefferson, Adams and Breckinridge; and the recently digitized papers of Kentucky's first attorney general, George Nicholas. Nicholas is also little known but was the founding genius of Kentucky's 1792 constitution and a close associate of Jefferson's. Documents from his papers, the papers of others and scholarly journals discussed in this book suggest a direct influence from Jefferson on the inclusion of separation of powers provisions in this constitution.

More recent history on the legacy of Jefferson's impact on Kentucky's constitution is informed by thousands of pages of digital material from more than eighteen years as general counsel to Governor Paul Patton, chief deputy attorney general of Kentucky and chief of staff to a member of Congress. This, for example, relates from contemporaneous notes a rare meeting of seven former governors of Kentucky and Patton in the Executive Mansion on state constitutional reform in 1999.

Likewise, this material details recent efforts to amend the constitution and supports policy wins in Kentucky during Governor Patton's tenure, such as higher education and criminal justice reform; it also details lost opportunities such as tax reform and a bargain with the General Assembly to trade by constitutional amendment establishment of annual legislative sessions in return for a two-thirds veto for the governor. This was a much-needed reform nearly secured that was lost in the end. With such examples in mind, this book is not so much a comprehensive history of Kentucky's constitution but rather a tale of its continuing relevance to our lives and political events.

Finally, this book seeks to demonstrate the good nature of many of our public servants, laboring under the guidance of Kentucky's constitution, and how they work across the aisle to achieve remarkable results, often out of public view. What Chief Justice Stephens did, for example, often behind the scenes with Governor Patton and others, to better Kentucky is a story worth telling. And it is particularly relevant when we seem inundated with stories of a divisive political culture.

It is this aggressive view of partisan politics that may be influencing young people to pass on careers in public service. Some opt for jobs in the private sector and have little notion of the legacy of our state constitution or Jefferson's influence on it. Others take jobs in the tech or service industries, on Wall Street or with other employers where the politics, while there, may not result in seemingly constant gridlock. It is my hope this book may demonstrate that public service can be a rewarding place of achievement individually and on behalf of the citizenry. It has been and can yet again be that way.

Several people assisted in this project whom I would like to thank for reviewing the manuscript, making good suggestions on structure and helpful edits. These include Sheryl Snyder, who wrote the foreword to this volume; Reb Brownell, who helped immeasurably; Keith Runyon, who was a relentless and careful editor; Emily Parento; J. David Niehaus; and longtime friends Sarah Jackson and Ellen Hesen. Each is an accomplished attorney or scholar published or experienced in the constitutional law doctrine of separation of powers.

I'm likewise thankful to my parents, Jo Ann and Denis Fleming, for encouraging my interest in history and politics, as well as to my daughter, Elizabeth Strimer; her husband, Luke; my grandchildren Esther and Amos; Ken and Ann Fleming; Lee and Katherine Cotton; and Caroline Fleming. Equal thanks go to Thai Le, who helped greatly with the book's images, and Bruce Greenstein for his support and good suggestions.

Finally, I am grateful to the Hanna Holborn Gray Special Collections Research Center at the University of Chicago Library for its assistance with and permission to use portions of the Reuben T. Durrett Collection of George Nicholas Papers and its guidance on these papers in relation to Thomas Jefferson.

Chapter 1

KENTUCKY'S CONSTITUTION

A Timeline of Early Development

DATE AND EVENT

1784

Kentucky's first constitutional convention is held in Danville, Kentucky. This begins a series of meetings over the next eight years setting forth the proposed structure of and the reasons for a government that was to represent the Commonwealth of Kentucky. Among the reasons indicated for statehood was a rumored incursion of Native Americans, with a need to organize militarily; the increase in population; and the challenges of being governed from Richmond, Virginia, which was over the Appalachian Mountains.

1792

After a series of smaller conventions, Kentucky adopts and publishes its first constitution in Danville, accepted by the U.S. Congress on June 1. This constitution includes a version of the separation of powers clauses Jefferson favored for inclusion in Virginia and likely Kentucky. George Nicholas and John Breckinridge purportedly met with Jefferson at Monticello prior to this convention to receive these provisions. Nicholas plays a leading role at this convention, and handwritten notes in his papers prepared for the meetings reflect the influence of Jefferson on the separation of powers doctrine and mention him by name.

1799

A second constitutional convention is held over a period of days in the new state capital of Frankfort, Kentucky. Changes are made in the document expanding the power of the governor, abolishing the state Electoral College by requiring the governor, state senators and other leaders to be directly elected and retaining the separation of powers provisions favored by Jefferson. Breckinridge is credited with a leading role in revising Kentucky's constitution at this convention and is referred to along with George Nicholas as a "Father of Kentucky's Constitution."

Chapter 2

JOHN BRECKINRIDGE AND THOMAS JEFFERSON

A Chronology of Key Dates and Events

JOHN BRECKINRIDGE, 1760–1806

1760
Born near Staunton, Virginia.

1763
James Breckinridge, brother of John Breckinridge, is born in Virginia, a later associate of Thomas Jefferson in founding the University of Virginia, member of Congress from Virginia and a general in the War of 1812.

1779–81
Attends College of William & Mary, Virginia. Studies law under George Wythe, is elected to the Virginia House of Delegates and most likely meets Thomas Jefferson.

1784
Marries Mary Hopkins Cabell and is admitted to practice law in Virginia.

1789–92
Visits Kentucky for the first time, gradually purchases 1,600 acres on North Elkhorn River and names his plantation Cabell's Dale in honor of his wife.

1792–95
Practices law in Virginia; moves to Kentucky and practices law. Purportedly meets with Jefferson and George Nicholas on Kentucky's

constitution. Is appointed attorney general of Kentucky under Governor Isaac Shelby.

1797–1805
Serves in Kentucky General Assembly, including as Speaker of the House. Introduces Kentucky Resolutions secretly written by Jefferson; serves prominently at Kentucky's 1799 constitutional convention. Practices law in Central Kentucky. The Alien and Sedition Acts are enacted by Congress in 1798. A protest against the Acts occurs, at which George Nicholas and Henry Clay speak.

1801–5
Serves as U.S. senator from Kentucky and spearheads Congressional approval of the Louisiana Purchase.

1805–6
Serves as attorney general of the United States under President Thomas Jefferson.

1806
Dies at Cabell's Dale, his plantation near Lexington, Kentucky, on December 14.

THOMAS JEFFERSON, 1743–1826

1743
Born in Shadwell, Virginia.

1760–65
Attends College of William & Mary, Virginia. Studies law under George Wythe, a founding father of the United States and signer of the Declaration of Independence.

1767–68
Is admitted to practice law in Virginia; is elected to Virginia House of Burgesses.

1772
Marries Martha Wayles Skelton.

1775–76
Is a delegate from Virginia to Second Continental Congress; drafts Declaration of Independence in Philadelphia.

1776–79
Is a member of the Virginia House of Delegates.

1779–81
Elected governor of Virginia; probable time of first meeting with John Breckinridge and George Nicholas.

1781–83
Elected delegate to the Continental Congress; British troops reach Monticello during their invasion of Central Virginia while Jefferson is the governor of Virginia.

1785–93
Serves as minister to France and first U.S. secretary of state; intermittently visits Monticello.

1797–1801
Serves as vice president under John Adams; secretly drafts the Kentucky Resolutions in response to the Alien and Sedition Acts and corresponds with Breckinridge, who is elected U.S. senator from Kentucky.

1801–9
Serves as president of the United States; appoints John Breckinridge attorney general. Breckinridge dies in 1806 outside Lexington, Kentucky.

1815
Sells his 6,700-volume library to Congress, establishing basis for the Library of Congress in Washington, D.C.

1825
The University of Virginia, which he founded, opens. James Breckinridge, brother of John Breckinridge, corresponds three times with Jefferson at Monticello.

1826
Dies at his home Monticello in Virginia on July 4; John Adams dies on the same day.

Chapter 3

THE BRECKINRIDGE FAMILY AND GEORGE NICHOLAS

*Kentucky's Connection to Thomas Jefferson
and the State Constitution*

John Breckinridge of Kentucky was born near Staunton, Virginia, in 1760 and served three terms in the Virginia House of Delegates beginning at age twenty. This apparently was illegal but overlooked at the time, as the minimum age to serve in this body was and remains twenty-one. His father, Robert Breckinridge, was the son of Scotch-Irish immigrants and served as a trustee for the then small town of Staunton in northwest Virginia. In 1763, Robert and his wife, Letitia, had a second son, James Breckinridge, who served in the Virginia House of Delegates, became a lawyer and later was a close associate of Thomas Jefferson's.[2]

Clearly, John Breckinridge was active politically before he moved to Kentucky. He was elected in 1780 to the Virginia House of Delegates first from Botetourt County southwest of Staunton, and later he represented nearby and newly formed Montgomery County. Both counties were highly rural and recently settled, bordering what became the states of Kentucky and West Virginia. Traveling what were great distances at the time, Breckinridge went back and forth between his home counties, where he was employed as a land surveyor, and the capitol in Richmond and briefly Williamsburg. In Williamsburg, he studied law at the College of William & Mary, this being where the legislature located during the Revolutionary War when the British invaded Virginia before retreating to Yorktown and surrendering. Breckinridge was astonished to have been elected to serve in the Virginia legislature and was barely twenty-one when he finally took his seat in 1781. Writing to his uncle at the time, he stated, "The confidence my acquaintances were pleased to repose in me does me the greatest honor and raises no small ambition in me to endeavor to serve them as well as I am capable of. As it is a post that I have the smallest knowledge of, and which I should imagine would require a good deal of prudence and caution.…I am afraid I shall be greatly at a loss for some time how to act comfortably to its rules."[3]

Breckinridge served in the Virginia legislature through 1785, when he was admitted to practice law in the state after intermittently completing his studies at William & Mary. Even at this young age, he seems to have been a polymath if not an intellectual of sorts despite a frontier existence. Here is a man who practiced law, wrote a book at the age of twenty-five on westward expansion and raised funds for a road connecting the Cumberland Gap to Central Kentucky, all before he moved to the state. As we shall see in the sixth chapter, this zeal for westward expansion was later tapped by Jefferson when he was president when he asked then U.S. senator from Kentucky John Breckinridge to navigate legal aspects of the Louisiana Purchase in 1803.

While it's obscured in history as to the genesis of the relationship between Breckinridge and Jefferson, it may very well have begun with connections at the College of William & Mary, where both studied under the preeminent American legal scholar of the time, George Wythe, as did Breckinridge's brother, James. Despite their differences in age, it's likely that he came across Jefferson while serving in the Virginia House of Delegates, where his colleagues included future Kentucky attorney general George Nicholas, several founding fathers of the nation and others prominent in business and legal affairs.[4] At the time Breckinridge took office in this body, Jefferson was serving as governor of Virginia (1779–81), having just completed three years of service in the House of Delegates (1776–79), and later served as Virginia's delegate to the Confederation Congress in 1782.

Also in 1784, Breckinridge became a charter member of a little discussed today but short-lived organization known as the Constitutional Society of Virginia. Formed in June of that year, it appears to have only met three times, with its purpose being to propose revisions to the Constitution of Virginia and for its members "to commit to paper our sentiments in plain and intelligible language on every subject which concerns the general will and transmit the same" among themselves.

The meetings of this society appeared to have been in Richmond or Williamsburg, and its members included Patrick Henry, James Madison, John Nicholas (brother of George Nicholas and Cary Nicholas), John Brown (later U.S. senator from Kentucky) and other associates of Thomas Jefferson's, some of whom became delegates to the first constitutional convention of the

United States in 1787. The apparent demise of this group was due to the exit of its founder, Filippo Mazzei, to Italy. Mazzei was an Italian intellectual who purchased land in Virginia from Thomas Jefferson and started a winery that failed shortly after the Revolutionary War. For our purposes, however, and as a charter member of this society, Breckinridge at age twenty-four was already showing keen interest in state constitutional development that later served him well in Kentucky.[5]

From his correspondence in the 1780s, Breckinridge seemed increasingly interested in moving west for economic reasons and to develop what he thought could be an opportunistic law practice. Also, his half-brothers Alexander and Robert Breckinridge had moved to Kentucky around 1781 and were writing to John Breckinridge of their newfound prosperity, enticing him to move there. Over a series of trips to Central Kentucky in the late 1780s, Breckinridge fell in love with the beauty of the area and began a series of land purchases along the North Elkhorn River that initially culminated in a plantation of more than 1,600 acres. This home, which stayed in the Breckinridge family for generations, was located strategically about six miles outside Lexington, Kentucky, where Breckinridge eventually established his law practice. The plantation was named Cabell's Dale, reflecting the maiden name of his wife, Mary Hopkins Cabell, whom he married in 1785.

The strong connections in Virginia, his public service and the beginnings of his law practice continued to delay the departure of Breckinridge to Kentucky in the early 1790s. Despite previous trips to the state and the incremental purchase of Cabell's Dale from 1789 to 1792, he remained active in Virginia politics; in February 1792, he was elected to Congress after being urged by colleagues to seek this office. Finding himself increasingly interested in settling in Kentucky and possibly at the urging of his wife, "Polly," whose mother and sister also had moved to the state, he resigned from Congress within a few months of his election.

About this time in 1792, Breckinridge and George Nicholas, who played a leading role in developing Kentucky's first constitution, purportedly met with Thomas Jefferson at Monticello in Virginia and discussed provisions that Jefferson encouraged them to include in this document. As we shall see, these clauses included the critical separation of powers clauses that eventually became Sections 27 and 28 of our current constitution and which Kentucky's Supreme Court has repeatedly stated were penned by Jefferson. Although Breckinridge, who had visited Kentucky several times and owned property in the state, was not present at Kentucky's 1792 constitutional convention, George Nicholas was present and took a leading role in constructing the document. Among the reasons indicated by Nicholas and others for Kentucky statehood was a rumored incursion of Native Americans into the territory, with the need to organize militarily; the increase in population; and the challenges of being governed from Richmond, Virginia, which was over the Appalachian Mountains nearly five hundred miles away.[6]

Nicholas is notable as following a similar path as Breckinridge, having studied law at the College of William & Mary under Wythe before serving in the Virginia House of Delegates from 1778 to 1788. Along with Breckinridge, who served in this body from 1781 to 1785, Nicholas almost certainly interacted with Thomas Jefferson, who served as governor of Virginia from 1779 through 1781. In 1780, following the death of his father, Nicholas left Williamsburg, Virginia, where he had been living, and moved to Charlottesville, Virginia. Monticello, the home of Jefferson, is less than four miles by road from Charlottesville.

This places Jefferson and Nicholas in proximity for several years and on familiar ground for the purported meeting at Monticello in 1792 on Kentucky's constitution. The correspondence of Jefferson in the summer and fall of 1792 reveals him to be traveling back and forth between Philadelphia and Monticello. Even Nicholas's younger brother, Cary, U.S. senator from Virginia (1799–1804) and governor of Virginia (1814–16), lived within eighteen miles of Jefferson and later lived less than a mile from Monticello on Tufton Farm, on land owned by Jefferson.[7]

George Nicholas eventually moved to Kentucky shortly before Breckinridge and purchased large tracts of land outside Danville, Kentucky, where he established farming operations. In 1789, in one of his first letters from Kentucky to his brother Cary, George Nicholas commented favorably on his new land purchases in Mercer, Fayette and part of Lincoln County. He was likewise positive as to the good prospects for "crops of corn, tobacco, flax and hemp" but noted that "parties run high here. I absolutely refuse to have anything to do with politics." He went on to urge his brother to purchase land nearby in Danville, but to not buy anything "until he has come and seen the country." Danville was the territory's first capital, and it was also the location of a series of constitutional conventions from 1784 through 1792, when Kentucky's first constitution was adopted under the leadership of George Nicholas. The farming prospects of Nicholas when he first arrived in Central Kentucky may have been good, but his refusal to get involved in politics was a premature decision.[8]

Before going to Kentucky, however, Nicholas was Jefferson's contemporary in the legal and governmental community of Virginia. He also appears to have corresponded often in the late 1780s with James Madison on matters related to early notions on Kentucky's constitution and Virginia's constitution, which Nicholas also worked on.[9] In reference to the service of Nicholas in the Virginia legislature in the 1780s, Jefferson noted in correspondence that Nicholas was a "very honest and able man," but also "young and ardent."[10]

In "The Political Ideas of George Nicholas," published in 1941 in the *Register of the Kentucky State Historical Society*, Huntley Dupre, PhD, professor of history at the University of Kentucky, delved into the association of Jefferson and Nicholas. In this well-supported article, Dupre wrote, "In the Virginia legislature George Nicholas became a leading supporter of Jefferson." He went on to say that, later, "Nicholas was a prominent and influential member of the Virginia Convention of 1788 to consider the federal Constitution. That Nicholas was steeped in the political philosophy of Jefferson and Madison…is demonstrated by his speeches at the convention," at which "Nicholas revealed his devotion to the principle of the separation of powers." Nicholas was later to apply his devotion to these principles in his work on Kentucky's first constitution in 1792.[11]

While Nicholas may have feigned an early objection to Kentucky politics, his chief interests in his new state soon became his law practice and his role in public life. He considered refusing but then accepted an appointment by President Washington to be the first U.S. attorney for the Kentucky District.[12] This put him squarely in the middle of state and national affairs, where he drew on his connections from Virginia politics to champion statehood for Kentucky. Nicholas became engaged in the early Danville meetings on a constitution for Kentucky, and at the April 1792 Danville Convention, he became the leading member of the committee to draft a constitution. One of the first articles of the new constitution contained the twin separation of powers provisions that the papers of Nicholas from this convention demonstrate were inspired by Thomas Jefferson.

In the Reuben Durrett Collection of George Nicholas Papers in the Hanna Holborn Gray Special Collections Research Center, University of Chicago Library, there is an interesting set of handwritten notes labeled "Writings-Notes-On a speech in favor of the Constitution circa 1792" (Series III-Writings, Box 1, Folder 9).[13] A page from these notes of Nicholas is reproduced in the illustrations, where almost the entire page is devoted to the separation of powers doctrine in the structure of Kentucky's constitution. At the bottom of this page is handwritten "Jefferson 195."

This may very well be a citation to page 195 of the 1787 London edition of Thomas Jefferson's *Notes on the State of Virginia*. On page 195 of this edition, reproduced in the illustrations, Jefferson wrote of the work at the Virginia constitutional convention in 1776, "…which passed this ordinance of government, laid its foundation on this basis, that the legislative, executive and judiciary departments should be separate and distinct, so that no person should exercise the powers of more than one of them at the same time." Jefferson's note on page 195 goes on to suggest that a distinct "barrier" between the branches of government was needed, otherwise "the judiciary and executive members were left dependent on the legislative, for their subsistence in office." As evidenced by the very label for this folder of notes and its contents, Nicholas appears to have used this material of Jefferson's on separation of powers doctrine in his work on Kentucky's 1792 constitution, where distinct separation of powers clauses were included. The Durrett Collection of the Nicholas Papers includes two original editions of Jefferson's *Notes*, the 1787 London edition and the 1792 Philadelphia edition.

While the handwriting on the page in the Nicholas Papers "Jefferson 195" and separation of powers notions looks different from others in this folder, it's conjecture as to who wrote it. Further, this page is the fourth of eight on the 1792 Kentucky Constitution, with the first four in different handwriting but with interlineations that almost certainly are by Nicholas. The final four pages in the folder look to be in the handwriting of Nicholas alone and deal with the formation of Kentucky's constitution. At one point, he appears to restate word for word portions from the first four pages that are in a different hand, which state the "Jefferson 195" citation and discuss powers of the branches of government.

This material in the Nicholas Papers may be a product of or related to the purported meeting of Nicholas, Breckinridge and Jefferson at Monticello in 1792 on Kentucky's constitution. Notably, Breckinridge made the long trip between Virginia and Kentucky several times from 1789 through 1793, often without his wife, traveling "widely over the central and northern parts of Kentucky, searching for the exact location which he wanted."[14]

As to whether the first four pages in the 1792 Nicholas folder may even be notes in Jefferson's handwriting or someone else's as a product of that reported meeting at Monticello, it is difficult to know. But Jefferson's name is clearly stated. In relevant parts on the third and fourth pages in this folder it states (emphasis added):

> *When the power of making, executing, and judging of the laws were all placed in the same hands, there would be no security for anything. As the same man might enact tyrannical laws, execute them in an arbitrary manner and then judge of them so as to justify his conduct.…*

*…but by separating them the legislator will not pass an improper act because another is to execute it and he is to be subject to it. The executive dare not act oppressively under it as another is to judge of his conduct and the judge will declare an unconstitutional law void and punish the executive officer for his tyranny.…***Such a government where powers are mixed possesses also the advantages and is clear of the evils of a monarchy. By dividing the power into different hands you are certain that one of them will oppose any improper step of the other.…**

…

Jefferson 195. Thus to have a good government… [see illustrations where this note from the Nicholas Papers and page 195 of Jefferson's *Notes on the State of Virginia* are reproduced].[15]

Other references to Jefferson in the handwriting of Nicholas regarding the doctrine of separation of powers and Kentucky's constitution appear in the digital records of the Nicholas Papers. In Box 1, Folder 16 of these papers labeled "Checks and Division of Powers," at the very end of an eight-page, single-spaced essay on the need for distinct separation between the branches of government is the notation "Jefferson 126.7 s." In one portion, Nicholas seems concerned with legislative encroachment on the executive, writing on page 4 of this folder, "Thus the legislature cannot transfer to themselves any of the branch of the executive powers."

There are other citations to "Jefferson 126" in the handwritten Nicholas Papers that appear to be a reference to page 126 of later edition of Jefferson's *Notes*. On this page, Jefferson recounted an episode from the 1776 Virginia constitutional convention where the House of Delegates proposed plenary power for the executive, "including every power legislative, executive and judicial, civil and military, of life and death." While the proposal was defeated, he went on to use this example as another reason to have balance in structure among the branches of government.[16]

We find another reference in the Nicholas Papers to the separation of powers doctrine, this time in a third box labeled "Speech in Kentucky Convention (circa 1792)." Presumably from these contemporaneous notes, this content may very well have been used by Nicholas at the 1792 Kentucky Constitutional Convention in Danville. This folder seems written in the style of a speech, and the last remark on the last page states, "To have a good government…you must provide material checks among the several departments of power; all power must be derived through different channels from the people and be distributed through different branches, each branch independent of the others and all dependent upon the people."[17]

Finally, throughout the boxes of Nicholas Papers are repeated handwritten references to "Montesquieu." Charles Montesquieu was the eighteenth-century French philosopher known as the source of the theory of separation of governmental powers and is referenced by Jefferson in his writings and in *The Federalist Papers* by Madison, John Jay and Alexander Hamilton. Often the Nicholas Papers cite Montesquieu in arguments related to separation of powers doctrine, even grouping a reference to "Montesquieu" next to one on Jefferson. While the papers are numerous, there are many handwritten references to Jefferson and Montesquieu throughout the papers of George Nicholas. It seems well supported that George Nicholas played a leading role at the Kentucky Convention of 1792, as evidenced by extensive handwritten notes he prepared for the meetings. These notes repeatedly cite the influence of Jefferson on the doctrine of separation of powers and mention Jefferson by name.[18]

While Nicholas was heavily engaged in developing the 1792 Kentucky Constitution in Danville, he seems not to have been present in Frankfort at the 1799 convention, possibly due to ill health; he died in June of that year at age forty-five. Despite health issues apparently due to his physical size, he managed to make an appearance in August 1798 to speak briefly in Lexington at the large rally in opposition to the Alien and Sedition Acts.[19] Just months before his death, Nicholas was appointed and served briefly as the first law professor at Transylvania University in Lexington, an institution that Breckinridge helped to establish. The connection of Nicholas to Breckinridge and Jefferson and in development of Kentucky's early constitution and its separation of powers provisions cannot be underestimated.

Regarding these separation of powers provisions, it's useful to point out the text of the lead paragraphs of Article I of this first 1792 Kentucky Constitution. These clauses were later retained in substance in 1799 at the convention at which Breckinridge took a leading role:

Article I of the First Constitution of Kentucky as Adopted in Danville, Kentucky in April of 1792

The powers of government shall be divided into three distinct departments, each of them to be confided to a separate body of magistracy, to wit: those which are legislative to one, those which are executive to another and those which are judiciary to another.

No person or collection of persons, being of one of these departments, shall exercise any power properly belonging to either of the others, except in the instances hereinafter expressly permitted.[20]

As we shall see, Kentucky's Supreme Court in published opinions not only traced the history of these provisions but also repeatedly took the position that Jefferson wrote them for Kentucky's constitution—and that this was a product of the political environment and the meeting at Monticello with John Breckinridge and George Nicholas on the subject. At that meeting in 1792, Jefferson purportedly warned them of the dangers of not including these provisions in their state constitution and thought that they should have been included in the federal Constitution. Certainly, George Nicholas seemed concerned of such dangers in his handwritten notes for the 1792 Kentucky Constitutional Convention that reference Jefferson repeatedly. Part of our story explores the philosophical underpinnings of Breckinridge that may have motivated him and George Nicholas to adopt Jefferson's suggestions and their lifetime of collaboration on similar matters, including the Kentucky Resolutions and even the Louisiana Purchase.[21]

BY THE SPRING OF 1793, after several trips to the state, Breckinridge was confident enough about his move to Kentucky to write to his good friend John Preston, a member of the Virginia House of Delegates and longtime treasurer of Virginia, "I am fixing fast for Kentucky: and shall be in perfect readiness by the time appointed. The opposition here is great; But I have reflected too long on the subject and am too firmly persuaded of its propriety to be shaken by any terrestrial mandate."[22]

Once in Kentucky, the promise of Breckinridge flowered even more when, as an attorney and then a member of the Kentucky House of Representatives, he took the lead in criminal justice reform modeling a new criminal code after efforts Jefferson had made in Virginia calling for rehabilitation of criminals and other reforms advanced for their time. The progressive notions of Breckinridge on criminal justice reform that he carried forward from Jefferson's proposed penal code for Virginia and that state's constitution are discussed further in the twelfth chapter in the context of modern reforms in Kentucky.

Breckinridge soon established a law office outside Lexington, Kentucky, not far from his home on the North Elkhorn River, and populated his office with books reputed to have been among the best law libraries in the area.

Wisely thinking ahead, Breckinridge purchased months before his departure more than 150 volumes, mostly history and legal texts, which he placed in luggage that traveled with him and his wife on the arduous journey to Central Kentucky.[23] Taking a northerly route through Pennsylvania, the couple made their way down the Ohio River, reaching Limestone Creek sixty-five miles outside Lexington before they finally arrived after a six-week journey.

Residing first in Lexington in 1793, the couple made plans to build a new residence at Cabell's Dale while Breckinridge developed his law practice. Kentucky had just been admitted to the Union in 1792, and Breckinridge and his wife found this to be a bustling community populated in part by recent immigrants. Like themselves, most had made the tough trip down the Ohio River or through the Cumberland Gap. As late as 1793, the year of their journey to Kentucky, there were still sporadic reports of attacks by Native Americans on settlers making their way down the Ohio River.[24] Repeatedly, many of these immigrants chose to settle in the lush countryside of Central Kentucky, the fast-developing town of Lexington or in Louisville, where the Falls of the Ohio made a natural break in river travel. By the time Breckinridge arrived in Kentucky with his family, he owned more than thirty thousand acres of land that he had gradually purchased beginning in 1789.

Breckinridge rapidly expanded his law practice, specializing in land disputes for which he was well trained in Virginia. He took an occasional criminal case, once representing an alleged horse thief and even a client threatened with hanging for counterfeiting state currency. By today's standards, his law office was modest and was in a small wood-frame building close to his home at Cabell's Dale.[25] Soon, Breckinridge began not only to practice law but also to teach it, using his new library as a source of knowledge for students. He quizzed them in a debating society he established by deploying a Socratic-style dialogue he learned studying law at William & Mary. This early but already profound interest of Breckinridge in educational matters spilled over later into his work as a trustee of what became Transylvania University in Lexington.[26]

Soon, he became more enmeshed in the politics of the state and Central Kentucky. In recognition of his legal brilliance and respect in the community, Kentucky's first governor, Isaac Shelby, appointed Breckinridge attorney general of the state in 1793, a position that he held through the end of 1797. Breckinridge was the second state attorney general; George Nicholas briefly served as the first in 1792. In a dizzying series of events, within weeks of this appointment in 1793, Breckinridge received an appointment by commission from President Washington and initialed by Jefferson, at that time U.S.

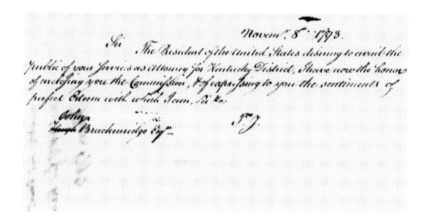

FIRST (PERMANENT) STATE HOUSE, FRANKFORT, KY.
(Built, 1793-94; and Destroyed by fire, Nov. 25, 1813.)

Top: November 1793 letter from Secretary of State Thomas Jefferson in which John Breckinridge is commissioned by President Washington "Attorney for the Kentucky District." *Library of Congress.*

Bottom: Kentucky's first capitol building in Frankfort—built in 1794, destroyed by fire in 1813. John Breckinridge served here during Kentucky's 1799 constitutional convention. *Kentucky Historical Society.*

[195]

4. All the powers of government, legislative, executive, and judiciary, result to the legislative body. The concentrating these in the same hands is precisely the definition of despotic government. It will be no alleviation that these powers will be exercised by a plurality of hands, and not by a single one. 173 despots would surely be as oppressive as one. Let those who doubt it turn their eyes on the republic of Venice. As little will it avail us that they are chosen by ourselves. An *elective despotism* was not the government we fought for; but one which should not only be founded on free principles, but in which the powers of government should be so divided and balanced among several bodies of magistracy, as that no one could transcend their legal limits, without being effectually checked and restrained by the others. For this reason that convention, which passed the ordinance of government, laid its foundation on this basis, that the legislative, executive and judiciary departments should be separate and distinct, so that no person should exercise the powers of more than one of them at the same time. But no barrier was provided between these several powers. The judiciary and executive members were left dependant on the legislative, for their subsistence in office, and some of them for their

O 2   continuance

Left: Page from Series III, Box 1, Folder 9, "Notes—On a speech in favor of the Constitution—circa 1792," George Nicholas Papers, University of Chicago Library. Note the text "Jefferson 195." *Reproduced with permission.*

Right: "195" likely refers to page 195 of the 1787 edition of Jefferson's *Notes on the State of Virginia*, on separation of powers in Virginia's constitution. *Library of Congress and Nicholas Papers.*

secretary of state, to be the U.S. attorney for Kentucky. Breckinridge would have been the top federal prosecutor in the state. Naturally, this was a time of no telephones, and with the delay in communications, Breckinridge, perhaps reluctantly, declined the appointment after he received it.

While Breckinridge admired Governor Shelby, Shelby was unable under Kentucky's constitution to run for reelection in 1797. A highly regarded firebrand, Shelby was a legendary leader of Patriot militia during the Revolutionary War and served a second term as governor from 1812 to 1816.[27] But in 1797, in a disputed election decided by a state Electoral College, James Garrard was elected governor over Benjamin Logan, a close friend of Breckinridge's.

This page: Nicholas Papers citing "Jefferson 126," "Montesquieu" and "Jefferson" Box 1, Folder 9, Notes—On a speech in favor of the Constitution—circa 1792. *Nicholas Papers, reproduced with permission.*

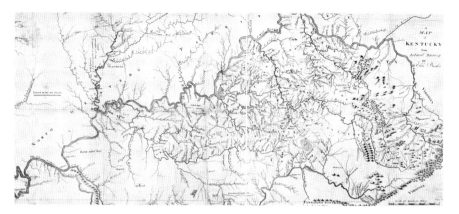

Map of Kentucky made in Philadelphia by Mathew Carey, 1793. Danville, site of the first constitutional convention, is southwest of Lexington. *Library of Congress.*

Apparently sour at the prospect of serving as attorney general under the new governor, Breckinridge resigned from his position and immediately won election to a vacant seat in Kentucky's General Assembly from the new county of Fayette. Breckinridge's bitterness over that election's outcome fueled his drive in 1799 to eliminate Kentucky's Electoral College, which resulted in the direct election of the position of governor and other state officials. Critically, Breckinridge played a leading role at the 1799 constitutional convention, which essentially retained the separation of powers clauses originally in the 1792 constitution. These clauses purportedly were received from Jefferson himself, potentially even in his own handwriting.

In 1798, however, a year before those constitutional developments in Kentucky, a bolt of lightning flashed across the new nation when Congress passed the Alien and Sedition Acts. That year, Breckinridge and Garrard found themselves united in furious opposition to this new federal law. It was about this time that Breckinridge, while on yet another trip back to Virginia, obtained a draft of legislation authored secretly by his good friend Thomas Jefferson that said states have the right to declare the Alien and Sedition Acts unconstitutional and invalidate them. Breckinridge later passed this legislation in the Kentucky General Assembly, which was the first of two declarations to be known as the Kentucky Resolutions and which are the centerpiece of the next chapter in our book.

Chapter 4

THOMAS JEFFERSON, JOHN BRECKINRIDGE AND THE ALIEN AND SEDITION ACTS

While somewhat lost in history to the public, the Kentucky Resolutions was a series of controversial provisions drafted in secret by Thomas Jefferson, introduced in the Kentucky House of Representatives by John Breckinridge with some edits and first enacted by the General Assembly in November 1798. Their relevance to our narrative is a critical demonstration of the connection between Breckinridge and Jefferson and the almost certain involvement of both men and George Nicholas in the early development of Kentucky's constitution.

The Kentucky Resolutions were incendiary documents for the time. They were instigated by the Alien and Sedition Acts, which empowered the president to deport aliens whom he considered a threat and even made it illegal to criticize the president or Congress. This set of laws was enacted by Congress in 1798, signed into law by President Adams and supported by the Federalist Party, which considered the bills a form of protectionism at the time the nation was in a developing naval war with France.

The new laws allowed the president not only to deport noncitizens but also to jail them if necessary; in the portion that angered Jefferson, they criminalized false statements about the government and the president himself. Another part of the law increased from five to fourteen years the time for naturalization and citizenship, which particularly irritated Irish immigrants, who were perceived at the time as being sympathetic to the French. These acts of Congress passed quickly in June and July 1798 as war fever gripped the nation.

This so-called Quasi-War with France was never declared and constituted a series of periodic naval engagements in the Caribbean starting in 1798. A primary cause of the dispute was the suspension by Congress of its obligation to repay loans the French had made to the United States during the American Revolutionary War. There were early, failed efforts to resolve the matter diplomatically. Congress took the position that the loans made by France during the Revolutionary War were not payable given the execution of Louis the XVI and establishment of the French First Republic in the early 1790s. Further, the United States felt it was insulted due to the recent XYZ Affair in which the French foreign minister allegedly demanded a cash bribe to deign to meet with envoys from America. "XYZ" was simply a substitute designation for the names of the three French diplomats alleged to have demanded bribes as a condition for negotiations with the Americans. Much of the reaction of President Adams and Congress in passing the Alien and Sedition Acts in 1798, and the opposition of Thomas Jefferson and Kentucky to these acts in the Kentucky Resolutions, was a result of this undeclared war growing out of the XYZ Affair.

One cannot help but marvel at the similarities to some of the political rhetoric we see on the national scene today from the right of the political spectrum, and at times the left, raising similar remedies for the deportation of immigrants crossing our borders. President Adams and members of his administration went about the business of putting together a list of people he proposed to deport, even though Adams never carried through on it. Great numbers of people who had immigrated recently to the United States at the time picked up their belongings and left the country for good. Given Jefferson's libertarian leanings, it is not surprising that he disagreed with the Alien and Sedition Acts strongly as violating the free speech provisions of the First Amendment, and likewise he probably saw the acts as a way politically by Adams's Federalist Party to advance their aims.

Other events from this time contributed to Jefferson's view that the Federalists under Adams were reactionary. Adams, with the encouragement of Alexander Hamilton and others known as High Federalists, pushed creation of a navy to deal with the French, a needed but costly step, while also greatly expanding the army hoping to raise twenty thousand men.[28] Then, to pay for it all, Congress enacted a series of federal property taxes that furthered protest if not outright rebellion throughout the nation.

The states were especially sensitive at this time over additional tax burdens, and recent rebellions were fresh in the minds of many. The violent Whiskey Rebellion in 1794 saw farmers in Western Pennsylvania revolt against a federal tax on spirits, and Shays's Rebellion before this in Massachusetts opposed a state tax to retire debt. The nation itself had been founded in part due to perceived grievances over taxes levied by the English Parliament without colonial representation.

In reaction to the Alien and Sedition Acts, Kentucky was one of the first states to boil over, but later again in Pennsylvania hundreds of farmers went through the roof. They took up arms. Under the command of John Fries, they forced the release of citizens jailed by the federal marshal for not paying the federally imposed property tax. President Adams arguably overreacted calling out federal troops to begin making arrests of those involved in the so-called Fries Rebellion, all of whom he later pardoned in 1800. It was in this volatile climate that Kentucky became a fulcrum for dissent for Jefferson and his Democratic-Republican Party.

In relation to our narrative and Kentucky, there was tremendous reaction against the Alien and Sedition Acts, particularly from the Democratic-Republican Party headed by Jefferson, who became president himself in 1800.[29] Once word circulated about the statute, which took several months, protests and demonstrations occurred across the nation, with one of the largest protests reported to have occurred in Lexington near the home of John Breckinridge and his family.

Newspapers of the time report that a young Henry Clay was a speaker at a raucous rally opposing these acts in the Cheapside area of downtown Lexington. Cheapside at this time was akin to Lexington's public square, and Clay's speech at this protest rally, attended by four to five thousand people, was well received. At the time, the population of Fayette County from the census in 1800 was a little over fourteen thousand, and more than a quarter of those were enslaved peoples. Clay and other speakers at the rally channeled the anti-Federalist mood of Kentucky.

This was but an early indication of great things to come politically for Henry Clay. Known as the "Great Compromiser" for his later work as a U.S. senator from Kentucky, Clay played a pivotal role in our nation's antebellum history and considered Lexington his home.[30] George Nicholas, essentially the father of the 1792 Kentucky Constitution, likewise spoke at this Lexington protest in opposition to the Alien and Sedition Acts less than a year before he died.[31] Later, in November 1798, the *Kentucky Gazette* reprinted a portion of Nicholas's town square remarks in apparent reference to the restrictions on free speech in the Alien and Seditions Acts:

As long as my country continues free, I care not who watches me: I wish all my thoughts, words and deeds so far as they concern the public, to be known. He who has not political objects, but the happiness and liberty of his country need not fear having them exposed to the eyes of the world. And if the time has come, when that liberty is to be terminated, I have lived long enough. Indeed, I have lived too long: if that be the case, it would have been better that I should have died before I became father of eleven children: and before I had instilled in them republican principles, which must add greatly to their wretchedness, if they are now to be slaves.[32]

The *Kentucky Gazette*, the state's preeminent newspaper of its time and the first founded west of the Allegheny Mountains, is filled in 1798 with stories about the outcry against the Alien and Sedition Acts. This paper was founded in 1787 by John and Fielding Bradford and began first as a weekly publication in Lexington. One edition published on August 1, 1798, reprinted as its lead article a speech delivered in Congress by Edward Livingston opposing the Alien and Sedition Acts. Livingston was a member of Congress from New York State and the younger brother of Robert Livingston, one of the founding fathers and a close associate of Thomas Jefferson's. In the lead article, the reporter said of Livingston that after being away from the House of Representatives a while, "he esteemed it one of the most fortunate occurrences of his life…that he had arrived in time to express his dissent to the passage of this bill."[33]

The *Kentucky Gazette* again reported the boiling sentiments against these acts in Lexington, Kentucky, in a front-page article about the huge protest assembly of August 15, 1798, where both Clay and Nicholas spoke. This story reprints in its entirety a resolution against the Alien and Sedition Acts and in support of the central Kentucky immigrant community. The resolution, as evidenced in the article, was apparently read to the crowd and was full of strong sentiment in opposition to these acts.[34]

Clay—who later developed a reputation as a somewhat hard-drinking, gambling but brilliant firebrand and distinguished statesman—was apparently roughed up by Federalist speakers at this Lexington rally who attempted to shout him down. It is conjecture as to whether John Breckinridge attended the rally in Lexington, but he was already established as a practicing lawyer with an office nearby. His attendance at the rally would seem more probable than not. Notably, biographies of Clay indicate that he had just relocated to Lexington in 1797, where he served an apprenticeship akin to a legal internship in the law office of John Breckinridge. Clay, like Breckinridge and

The *Kentucky Gazette* printed the speech of Congressman Edward Livingston of New York opposing Alien and Sedition Acts, August 1798. *Lexington, Kentucky Public Library Digital Collection.*

Thomas Jefferson before him, had studied law at William & Mary under George Wythe before moving to Kentucky.[35]

The Alien and Sedition Acts were the last straw for many citizens, who resented the perceived attack on immigrants recently located in the nation and throughout Kentucky. Emigrated citizens of recent Scotch-Irish descent, of which Breckinridge was one, and others considered sympathetic to the interests of France, with whom the nation was in an undeclared naval war, were targeted for unjustifiable ridicule. Jefferson was incensed at these new laws, describing them as "palpably in the teeth of the constitution" (i.e., unlawful) and referred to this time under President Adams as a "reign of witches."[36]

LONDON, May 21.

PARIS, May 12.

BERLIN, May 1.

FRANKFORT, April 28.

NEW-YORK, July 28.

NEWBURY-PORT, July 17.

CHARLESTON, July 18.

PHILADELPHIA, July 26.

Department of State,
July 21, 1798.
JACOB WAGNER, chief clk.

LANCASTER, July 28.

From the Aurora.

GEORGE-TOWN, July 27.

ALEXANDRIA, July 17.

Lexington, August 19.

Opposite: *Kentucky Gazette* reporting Lexington, Kentucky protest against the Alien and Sedition Acts, August 1798. *Lexington, Kentucky Public Library Digital Collection.*

Right: Photo of the law office of John Breckinridge, outside Lexington, Kentucky, built circa 1793. *Filson Historical Society online catalogue.*

Kentucky's sensitivities to the Alien and Sedition Acts are reflected in the state's generally pro-French sentiments, with many French-derived names and references among many counties, cities and towns in the state. All of this likely was a reflection of the great contributions France made to the nation in securing its independence through the Revolutionary War. Fayette County, for example, of which Lexington is the seat, founded in 1780, was named in honor of the Marquis de Lafayette, the great French statesman, friend of Jefferson and Revolutionary War general. Ironically, it was Lafayette who was assigned by George Washington to lead troops to thwart the invasion of the British in Central Virginia shortly before their surrender at Yorktown in 1781. Banastre Tarleton, the ruthless British cavalry officer, went as far as Monticello and occupied it briefly after Jefferson, who was governor of Virginia at the time, fled with hours to spare.[37]

Lafayette visited Kentucky in 1821 at the age of sixty-four, stopping in Louisville, then the Frankfort home of former U.S. senator John Brown, and finally in Lexington in the county named for him decades before. The county seat of Bourbon County, established in 1795, is Paris, and the county seat of Woodford County, established in 1788, is Versailles. What became the state's largest city, Louisville, was chartered in 1780 and named after King Louis XVI, who was executed during the French Revolution.

In the year 1798 alone, the *Kentucky Gazette* reported frequently on its front page the news, political or otherwise, from France, which itself had been in a state of revolution for years and was about to enter a period of rule by Napoleon Bonaparte. Given these close connections to France, it may be understandable that the politics of Kentucky at the time were suspicious of the actions of President Adams and Congress in opposition to the very country that helped the United States come into existence.[38]

Events in Kentucky in late 1798 continued to reach a boiling point. The governor of Kentucky, James Garrard, in a November 7 address before the General Assembly, reflected the mood of the state when he said that Kentucky "being deeply interested in the conduct of the national government, must have a right to applaud *or to censure that government* when applause or censure becomes its due" (emphasis added). He continued his remarks to reference with distaste the Alien and Sedition Acts, stating that Kentucky was a place "if not in a state of insurrection, yet utterly disaffected to the federal government." Kentucky was about to convert its dissent into action.[39]

Chapter 5

JOHN BRECKINRIDGE
AND THE KENTUCKY RESOLUTIONS

Why Jefferson Kept His Authorship a Secret

Shortly thereafter, Kentucky governor Garrard appointed Breckinridge chairman of a three-person committee that would prepare legislation, which had been secretly written by Jefferson himself, providing Kentucky the option to simply ignore federal law, including the Alien and Sedition Acts, and call on Congress to repeal them. This committee seems to have acted quickly, as the Kentucky Resolutions were brought to the floor of the General Assembly's House of Representatives on November 10, 1798. The Resolutions passed easily in that chamber and then passed the Senate and were signed by Governor Garrard. Breckinridge introduced the Resolutions, delivered the first-floor speech in the House in support of them and led the fight for passage.

Although several Federalist supporters of President Adams are recorded as offering floor speeches in opposition to the Resolutions, they were drowned out in the end. Only one vote was recorded as opposing the Resolutions in the House. Later in 1799, the Kentucky General Assembly, after several other states had rejected passage of similar legislation, passed a similar version of what passed in 1798. This version was seen essentially as a defense of the first enactment.

What the Kentucky Resolutions did, as did a similar measure written by Madison for Virginia, was to declare that the state could simply nullify or obviate federal laws or actions they considered unconstitutional. Both Resolutions received no support from the other states and were part of a political backdrop remarkably like what we experience in our divisive politics today. Some states such as New Hampshire considered the Resolutions an outright form of rebellion. Portions of the 1798 Resolutions, comprising nine sections, were apparently watered down at the end, with two of the provisions written by Jefferson empowering the state to nullify federal law being softened at the last minute.

Dumas Malone, in his Pulitzer Prize–winning six-volume series *Jefferson and His Time*, suggests that it most likely was Breckinridge who modified and even deleted certain passages proposed by Jefferson. Some provisions apparently were deleted as being repetitious, while others were omitted, including a stark declaration that "where powers are assumed which have not been delegated [to the federal government] a nullification of the act is the rightful remedy." Ironically, a modified nullification provision was added to the Resolutions by the Kentucky General Assembly in 1799 under the auspices of Breckinridge in response to other states that criticized the Resolutions and refused to consider them.

Malone also suggests that the actual delivery of the draft Resolutions from Jefferson to Breckinridge may have been done through Cary Nicholas (1761–1820), brother of George Nicholas, who was a member of the Virginia House of Delegates, then U.S. senator and governor of Virginia. Cary Nicholas also served with distinction in the Revolutionary War, rising to command George Washington's Life Guard, and was later instrumental in helping Jefferson establish the University of Virginia.[40]

The involvement of Nicholas with the Kentucky Resolutions seems confirmed in an October 5, 1798 letter from Jefferson to Nicholas less than six weeks prior to their first passage in Kentucky in 1798. Nicholas then lived on a homestead on the James River he called Mount Warren, less than eighteen miles from Monticello. This letter is one of several at this time between Nicholas and Jefferson and is notable for mentioning Breckinridge and offering a brief history of this initiative:

To Wilson Cary Nicholas
Monticello Oct. 5.98

Dr. Sir—I entirely approve of the confidence you have reposed in Mr. Breckinridge, as he possesses mine entirely. I had imagined it better those resolutions should have originated with N. Carolina. But perhaps the late changes in their representation may indicate some doubt whether they could have passed. In that case it is better they should come from Kentucky. I understand you intend soon to go as far as Mr. Madison's. You know of course I have no secrets from him. I wish him therefore to be consulted as to these resolutions. The post boy waiting at the door obliges me to finish here with assurances of the esteem of Dr. Sir your friend & servt.

Th. Jefferson[41]

As can be seen from this letter, Cary Nicholas was apparently a courier not only between Breckinridge and Jefferson on the Kentucky Resolutions but also with Madison, who was working on a similar version for passage by the Virginia General Assembly. The next month, Jefferson again wrote to Nicholas, this time in response to his examination of a draft of the Virginia Resolutions that Madison had left Nicholas for presentation to the Virginia legislature. This letter provides insight to Jefferson's great attention to detail in the drafting of legislation:

To Wilson Cary Nicholas
Nov. 29.98

The more I have reflected on the phrase in the paper you showed me, the more strongly I think it should be altered. Suppose you were to instead of the invitation to cooperate in the annulment of the acts, to make it an invitation: "to concur with this Commonwealth in declaring, as it does hereby declare that the said acts are, and were ab initio null, void and of no force, or effect" I should like it better. Health happiness and adieu.

Th. Jefferson[42]

Nicholas went on to incorporate Jefferson's suggestion for change, and the resolutions in Virginia were introduced by Representative John Taylor on December 10 and published in a Philadelphia newspaper, the *Aurora*, on December 22. Ultimately, the Virginia House of Delegates removed Jefferson's proposal and passed the resolutions more in line with Madison's temperate language. These letters from Jefferson to Nicholas are an insight not only to the role of Nicholas in working with Jefferson legislatively but also on his meticulous attention to phraseology and the impact of language. Still later, in September 1799, he wrote to Nicholas again on revisions to the Resolutions Kentucky was about to consider in reaction to their first passage in 1798. Nicholas was about to travel to Kentucky to handle the affairs of his brother George Nicholas, who passed away unexpectedly in

July of that year. Jefferson declined to offer further revisions but urged "a concert to the general plan of action" for Kentucky and Virginia "to pursue the same track on this occasion" in terms of the content of the legislation.

He closed out the letter saying, "Besides, how could you better while away the road from hence to Kentucky, than in meditating this very subject, and preparing something yourself, than whom nobody will do it better. The loss of your brother [George Nicholas]…excites anxiety."[43] This series of events and correspondence raises the question: could Cary Nicholas as a young lawyer have been a courier in 1792 between his brother George, Jefferson and Breckinridge in conveying text for inclusion in Kentucky's first constitution?

Jefferson himself was later embarrassed to have written the Kentucky Resolutions or was perhaps operating furtively. His preparation of them was known to very few at that time, excepting Breckinridge, the Nicholas brothers and Madison, because Jefferson was serving as Adams's vice president and could have been charged with treason or sedition for what he had done. Notably, the Resolutions prepared by Jefferson for Kentucky and as introduced and passed with the hard work of Breckinridge were even bolder than what Madison had prepared for Virginia.

In November 1798, Jefferson sent Madison a private letter enclosing a "draught of the Kentucky resolves," perhaps as a template for Madison to use in Virginia's resolutions, which passed in December 1798. Jefferson somewhat covertly suggested that they "leave the matter in such a train as that we may not be committed absolutely to push the matter to extremities, & yet may be free to push as far as events will render prudent."[44]

The Kentucky Resolutions stated in their key section that if the federal government "assumes undelegated powers, its acts are unauthoritative, void and of no force." Plainly, Breckinridge, based on his already long-standing friendship with Jefferson, was in part a vehicle for the anonymous outrage of Jefferson at the Alien and Sedition Acts, if not at President Adams himself. Jefferson at the time and later by his own admission recognized the dubious nature of the Kentucky Resolutions in the face of the Supremacy Clause under Article 6 of the U.S. Constitution. This clause expressly provides that states have no power to block enforcement of federal laws that in any event are subject to interpretation by the federal court system.

Holdings of the National Archives confirm development of the friendship among Breckinridge and Thomas Jefferson at this time in several letters from Jefferson, with some replies by Breckinridge also preserved. Two of these letters were written in January and February 1800 and were sent to Breckinridge via the postmaster in Louisville, Kentucky. One concerned

Jefferson's proposal, while he was vice president, to create a separate judicial district in "the West" where Breckinridge resided, and another notably referenced the version of the Kentucky Resolutions solely adopted in that state. Jefferson at this time was less than one year from assuming the presidency, and in early 1800, the famous portrait of Jefferson by Rembrandt Peale was completed.

Jefferson's letter to Breckinridge in January 1800 is worth reproducing in part because it is a rare reference in writing to the Kentucky Resolutions written directly to the chief sponsor of these provisions in the Kentucky General Assembly. This letter seems to have been written only a few months after Kentucky passed its 1799 version of the Resolutions, which added that states may nullify or declare as void any federal law a state deems unconstitutional. Interestingly, a footnote to this letter in the National Archive's online records indicate that in his own hand, Jefferson canceled out the words "alien &…," almost certainly a reference that he wished to avoid in writing as to the reason for these resolutions, the controversial Alien and Sedition Acts.

Following is the text of a letter from Jefferson to John Breckinridge in January 1800, referencing the Kentucky Resolutions (emphasis added):

Dear Sir,

Your favor of the 13th has been duly received, as had been that covering the resolutions of your legislature on the subject of the former resolutions. I was glad to see the subject taken up, and done with so much temper, firmness and propriety. from the reason of the thing I cannot but hope that the Western country will be laid off into a separate Judiciary district. *from what I recollect of the dispositions on the same subject at the last session, I should expect that the partiality to a general & uniform system would yield to geographical & physical impracticability. I was once a great advocate for introducing into Chancery vivâ voce testimony, & trial by jury. I am still so as to the latter; but have retired from the former opinion on the information received from both your state & ours, that it worked inconveniently. I introduced it into the Virginia law, but did not return to the bar, so as to see how it answered. but I do not understand how the vivâ voce examination comes to be practiced in the Federal court with you, & not in your own courts; the federal courts being directed by law to proceed & decide by the laws of the states.*[45]

Left: Rembrandt Peale portrait of Thomas Jefferson from life in 1800, just before he was first elected president of the United States. *Public domain.*

Right: Wilson Nicholas portrait by Gilbert Stuart, 1805. Nicholas was in the Virginia House of Delegates and was a U.S. senator, the governor of Virginia and brother of George Nicholas, the "father of Kentucky's Constitution." *Public domain.*

The modern-day application of the larger question posed by Jefferson in these little-known resolutions in Virginia and Kentucky, written by Madison and Jefferson respectively, has more than ample application to our national political life. State and federal courts, Congress and even state legislatures continue to struggle with this delicate balance between states' rights and our federal Constitution. This is evidenced in the foreign policy area in terms of the War Powers Act, for example, which is an effort to curb the powers of the presidency by Congress, and Kentucky's struggles as detailed in this book among the three branches of government. Even recent events reflect this dynamic in legal challenges to the powers of the states to remove a presidential candidate from their state ballots in relation to the U.S. Constitution's Fourteenth Amendment Insurrection Clause.

The Alien and Sedition Acts died a slow death by popular opinion, which in part was aided by Jefferson's secret work with Kentucky writing the Resolutions. While the law was never tested in court, it stirred deep emotions and seems to have been a victim of popular uprising. In a notable footnote to history, Justice William O. Douglas of the U.S. Supreme Court mentioned the Alien and Sedition Acts in a concurring opinion in *Watts v. United States*

Monticello, home of Thomas Jefferson outside Charlottesville, Virginia. Jefferson designed the building and was buried at the Monticello Cemetery after his July 4, 1826 death. *Library of Congress.*

(1966), which concerned a First Amendment issue involving threats against then President Lyndon B. Johnson.

Watts presented the interesting case of an eighteen-year-old Vietnam War protester who, after he had received his draft card at the induction center, made an offhand threat of violence with a firearm against President Johnson. He was prosecuted and convicted of violating a federal law prohibiting threats against the president, but in a 5-4 decision, the Court protected the speech of Watts, deeming it political hyperbole rather than an actual threat. In his concurring opinion, Douglas referenced the already ancient Alien and Sedition Acts and stated, "The Alien and Sedition Laws constituted one of the sorriest chapters; and I had thought we had done with them forever.... Suppression of speech as an effective police measure is an old, old device outlawed by our Constitution."[46]

Chapter 6

JEFFERSON'S TOP LAWYER

John Breckinridge as U.S. Senator, Attorney General
of the United States and His Untimely Death

The remarkable career of John Breckinridge continued to blossom in Kentucky, where his interest in constitutional matters remained strong. Since the adoption of Kentucky's constitution in 1792, and particularly given Breckinridge's bad experience with the governor's election by an Electoral College in 1797, voices across the state began to clamor for the calling of a constitutional convention, which occurred in 1799. His good sense, deep legal knowledge and popularity from having reformed Kentucky's penal system and from championing passage of the Kentucky Resolutions enhanced his reputation as a leader for constitutional reform.

Although the 1799 Kentucky Constitution is regarded as containing some regressive policy provisions, the document was amended to provide for legislative district apportionment based on population, to add a lieutenant governor of the state as a new office and, importantly, to eliminate the Electoral College, which had chosen state senators and the governor. Going forward, these positions were filled by direct election.

Despite a good deal of debate on the subject, the pro-enslavement provisions of the 1792 constitution were regrettably carried forward in 1799. Several structures for the emancipation of enslaved peoples were discussed but ultimately not recognized in the final document. This was despite the effort Reverend David Rice of Central Kentucky and other clergymen led in opposition to enslavement at the 1792 convention and in the following years.

Kentucky historian Lowell Harrison in his 1959 treatise *John Breckinridge and the Kentucky Constitution of 1799* characterized the debate regarding this constitution as being one that questioned the need to have a convention at all. Harrison suggested that Breckinridge and others were large property owners who represented an aristocratic element of planters and businessmen who clashed with settlers, "who occupied the worst of lands or had been pushed onto the barrens of the Green River country." It appears that the property owners represented by Breckinridge and others may have opposed the 1799 convention largely because they feared that enslavement, which was open to attack on moral and humanitarian grounds, might be subject to a process of emancipation if not abolition. While the convention ultimately resulted in several political reforms for Kentucky, enslavement continued in Kentucky for many decades as a blot on its history.[47]

Clearly, Breckinridge played the leading role in constitutional reform in 1799 and was mindful of the need to retain in the constitution the separation of powers provisions Jefferson likely urged for inclusion in state constitutions such as Kentucky's. Breckinridge was a particularly staunch defender of the state judicial system and mindful of the need to preserve the independence of this critical branch of state government. He defeated efforts by other members at the convention that would have given the state legislature the right to veto decisions of the state judiciary. As we shall see, with the leadership of Breckinridge at this 1799 convention, the revised constitution retained the separation of powers clauses that became Sections 27 and 28 of this document.

Riding a tide of popularity and acknowledged leadership, Breckinridge, who had recently been elected Speaker of the Kentucky House, was reelected Speaker in 1800, only to be proposed as a candidate for the U.S. Senate that same year. Unlike changes they had just made in the Kentucky Constitution for direct election of the governor and other state office holders, members of the Kentucky General Assembly still retained the power to select the state's two U.S. senators. In November 1800, the General Assembly nominated Breckinridge as a candidate and elected him the new U.S. senator from Kentucky over John Adair by a vote of sixty-eight to thirteen.[48]

That same year of his election to the Senate, the seventh of nine children was born to Breckinridge and his wife, Polly. His name was Robert Jefferson, perhaps reflecting the close association of Breckinridge and Jefferson through the years beginning with their work in the Virginia House of Delegates. Needing to wrap up pending affairs in Kentucky, particularly with his legal office, and in some cases turning over matters of legal representation to his associate Henry Clay, Breckinridge did not make it to Washington, D.C., until late in 1801.

As a member of the Senate in Washington, he renewed his close association with President Jefferson and became a champion of westward expansion of the nation. This goal became frustrated in 1802 when Spain revoked Kentucky's "right of deposit" in New Orleans, which was the state's right to use this port to store goods for transfer up the Mississippi River to states west of the Appalachian Mountains. While navigation on the river was not halted entirely, this was an aggressive move by Spain, which had agreed by treaty in 1795 for the western states to use the waterway. Some in Congress worried that military action to secure the right of deposit may be needed, but Jefferson and Breckinridge counseled diplomacy despite the uproar the actions of Spain created in Kentucky. Fortunately, in late 1802, the ambassador of the United States to France advised Jefferson that Spain had ceded the Louisiana Territory to France, which in turn was open to sell the land for the right price.[49]

Jefferson relied on Breckinridge for legal advice in 1803 as to the proper way to secure the Louisiana Purchase from France, which he felt Congress must empower him to do, fearing that to do so unilaterally was unconstitutional. This was a critical moment in the nation's history, as the Louisiana Purchase brought more than eighty-three thousand square miles of territory within the country that in time would encompass fifteen states.

In a letter to Breckinridge in August 1803, and in a sign of respect for his friend's legal mind despite Breckinridge being a new member of the Senate, Jefferson stated his concerns about whether the Constitution empowered the president unilaterally to acquire land from foreign nations. Although new states could be admitted to the Union by Congress under Article IV, Sec. 3 of the Constitution, Jefferson as a strict constructionist worried that nothing in the nation's charter specifically addressed acquisition of territories. Therefore, he was concerned that purchase of the Louisiana Territory comprising millions of acres with such a diverse population was a step too big for him to take. Having negotiated the treaty of purchase for the then tremendous sum of $15 million, which was nearly twice the size of the nation's budget at the time, Jefferson in his long letter to Breckinridge laid out his concerns and expressed anxiety over the whole affair.[50]

Jefferson already was familiar with the volatile nature of French politics, having served as United States minister to France. Relations were now complicated because he was dealing with the mercurial Napoleon Bonaparte, who had dramatically seized power in France. Learning that Napoleon might be open to selling this territory to the United States, Jefferson sent James Monroe in 1803 along with one of the founding fathers, Robert Livingston, to negotiate the sale. To the surprise of Monroe, who had leeway only to spend $10 million to acquire the territory, Napoleon wanted $22 million. After some tense negotiations, a deal was struck for the $15 million purchase.

Months went by before the news officially reached President Jefferson in Washington in July 1803. The president wrote to Breckinridge on August 12, 1803, with a sense of urgency, imploring his trusted friend to return to Washington to address issues related to the purchase before a late October deadline for ratification by Congress. Jefferson wrote (emphasis added):

> *This treaty must of course be laid before both Houses because both have important functions to exercise respecting it. They, I presume, will see their duty to their country in ratifying & paying for it, so as to secure a good which would otherwise probably be never again in their power. But I suppose they must then appeal to the nation for an additional article to the Constitution, approving & confirming an act which the nation had not previously authorized. The constitution has made no provision for our holding foreign territory, still less for incorporating foreign nations into our Union. The Executive in seizing the fugitive occurrence which so much advances the good of their country, have done an act beyond the Constitution. The Legislature in casting behind them metaphysical subtleties, and risking themselves like faithful servants, must ratify & pay for it, and throw themselves on their country for doing for them unauthorized what we know they would have done for themselves had they been in a situation to do it. It is the case of a guardian, investing the money of his ward in purchasing an important adjacent territory; & saying to him when of age, I did this for your good; I pretend to no right to bind you: you may disavow me, and I must get out of the scrape as I can: I thought it my duty to risk myself for you. But we shall not be disavowed by the nation, and their act of indemnity will confirm & not weaken the Constitution, by more strongly marking out its lines.....**I hope yourself and all the western members will make a sacred point of being at the first day of the meeting of Congress; for your interests are involved.** Accept my affectionate salutations and assurances of esteem and respect Th. Jefferson.*[51]

Breckinridge at first shared Jefferson's concern as to the constitutionality of the Louisiana Purchase, perhaps out of deference if not from a congenitally similar legal mindset both men had toward constitutional constructions and the need for explicit authority. This is precisely the dynamic both men shared in promoting explicit language in constitutional structures. This included the separation of powers provisions Jefferson favored among state constitutions and the detail both men included, albeit Jefferson secretly, in the Kentucky Resolutions.

But as a new member of the Senate from Kentucky, which at that time was perceived as being the Far West of the nation, Breckinridge developed a reputation of advocacy for western expansion and the construction of infrastructure to connect the growing populace. Breckinridge finally arrived back in Washington in mid-October after the long trip from Kentucky and began to meet with his Senate colleagues, with Jefferson, his cabinet and others on the subject.

Given the enormous stakes for the nation and with the Federalists on board with the purchase, Jefferson became relieved to learn that Breckinridge and his Senate colleagues were ready to proceed with ratifying the treaty for the Louisiana Purchase. It was Breckinridge himself on October 17 who introduced legislation authorizing President Jefferson to take possession of the Louisiana Territory, and following only three days of debate, on October 22, the Senate voted for ratification twenty-four to seven. The treaty was signed by Jefferson just in time on October 31, 1803.[52]

As an interesting footnote to the Louisiana Purchase and the teamwork of Breckinridge and Jefferson, evidently Jefferson became apologetic if not thankful for the work of Breckinridge in having his legal concerns resolved and legislation approving the purchase expedited. In a letter to Breckinridge on November 24, 1803, President Jefferson began the correspondence, which concerned several unrelated matters, with the sentence, "Dear Sir, I thought I perceived in you the other day a dread of the job of preparing a constitution for the new acquisition." This would suggest that Breckinridge was certainly less than favorable to the notion of amending the Constitution to empower the president to initiate the purchase of a foreign territory. Another more probable reading of this is that Jefferson was referring to the need to draft a territorial constitution to govern the Louisiana Purchase. The nation now possessed it but had to determine how best to govern it.[53]

Finally, the wisdom of these actions and the legal acumen of Breckinridge and others in relying on the treaty clause in the U.S. Constitution to affect the Louisiana Purchase was validated years later in a decision by the U.S. Supreme Court. This landmark decision was written by the Court's chief justice, John Marshall, who happened to be a cousin of Jefferson's. Marshall, in the 1823 decision *American Insurance Company v. Canter*, stated, "The Constitution confirms absolutely on the government of the union the powers of making war and of making treaties: consequently, that government possesses the power of acquiring territory, either by conquest or by treaty."[54]

Evidently deploying the same skills of attention to detail, great legal knowledge and camaraderie with his colleagues, Breckinridge soon became a leader in the Senate, focusing on matters of westward expansion and development of the new nation. Earlier in 1803, he had even been considered briefly by Jefferson's associates to be a candidate for vice president. In late 1805, Breckinridge only reluctantly left the Senate to accept appointment as U.S. attorney general when Jefferson asked that he do so following the resignation of Levi Lincoln from that position for unspecified personal reasons. This may be considered a controversial appointment given the invaluable skills of Breckinridge in the Senate in moving passage of Jefferson's priority legislation. Breckinridge was forty-four at this time and arguably at the peak of his career politically and legally.

A clue to Jefferson's political thinking in appointing Breckinridge may be gleaned from an August 7, 1805 letter the president wrote the Kentuckian from Monticello (emphasis added):

> *The Office of Attorney General for the U.S. being not permanently filled; I have an opportunity of proposing it for your acceptance....I shall with the greatest pleasure learn that you accede to my wishes in availing the public of your services,* ***as your geographical position will enable you to bring into our councils a knowledge of the western interests and circumstances for which we are often at a loss and sometimes fail in our desires to promote them.***[55]

Jefferson's hope to expand westward was demonstrated by his teamwork with Breckinridge on the Louisiana Purchase. This long-standing focus of Breckinridge in development of the western states played a critical role in his appointment. Both men likewise shared a keen interest in securing unfettered access to the vital Mississippi River and the navigational heart of the nation.

The tenure of Breckinridge as U.S. attorney general was short; his chief duties entailed representing the nation in cases before the U.S. Supreme Court. Several cases were ones he inherited from his predecessor, and while it appears he lost more cases than he won, he was notable for issuing several legal opinions. Among these was one questioning the City of New Orleans's effort to tax property belonging to the federal government within its jurisdiction. In advising that it was unconstitutional for the city to tax

Left: Portrait by Alban Conant of U.S. Attorney General John Breckinridge of Kentucky at the Department of Justice, Washington, D.C. *Public domain.*

Right: Kentucky's first governor, Isaac Shelby, by Matthew Jouett, circa 1820. Shelby was a Revolutionary War hero and governor (1792–96, 1812–16). *Library of Congress.*

federal property, the view of Breckinridge was validated later by the high court in 1819 in the landmark case *McCullough v. Maryland*.

A further window into the duties of Breckinridge as attorney general is evident in his correspondence. Often, he is replying to inquiries from members of the Senate and even Jefferson himself as to what he thinks of drafts of legislation. In one instance, Jefferson wrote to him in 1806, "What think you of the enclosed proposition?" Other letters from Jefferson or the president's assistant asked the attorney general to join a cabinet meeting to discuss North African affairs, and afterward Jefferson asked for "the favor to dine with him." Often good wine was served by his valet, with dinner prepared by Jefferson's chef, both of whom were French.

Other notes are less formal, including one a week after the North African affairs meeting in which Jefferson tells Breckinridge that he and Secretary of the Treasury Albert Gallatin are walking over to James Madison's office to discuss an "important and pressing subject." He asks his Kentucky friend, "Can you meet us there and amuse yourself till Mr. Gallatin comes, the moment of which I am not able to fix."[56] It seems certain that the judgment of Breckinridge, his friendship and legal acumen were valued deeply by one of the greatest presidents in our history.

In his correspondence from the early 1800s, Breckinridge complained of physical maladies and pulmonary difficulties that were ill defined. On a trip to Cabell's Dale in the spring of 1806, he became ill. Between bouts of sickness and recovery for the next few months, he wrote to Jefferson apologizing for his delay in returning to Washington. Unable to overcome whatever it was that had stricken him, Breckinridge died at his Kentucky home on Sunday, December 14, 1806, just as he was attempting to get his affairs in order to return to Washington. John Breckinridge was only forty-six years old at the time of his death.[57] But his work as a confirmed state constitutionalist and reformer, his role in passage of the Kentucky Resolutions proposed by Jefferson and his understanding of separation of powers doctrine as favored by Jefferson were only beginning to benefit Kentucky.[58]

Chapter 7

JEFFERSON'S FRIENDSHIP WITH THE BRECKINRIDGE FAMILY AND ITS LEGACY

In a little-known footnote to history, Joseph Cabell Breckinridge, the son of John Breckinridge, who had so famously served Kentucky and the nation, wrote a letter to Jefferson in 1821. In this letter, he asked Jefferson, who was seventy-eight at the time, if he was the author of the Kentucky Resolutions and if he was the conduit for them through his father. Jefferson replied in a letter of December 11, 1821, indicating that "by virtue of the specific question posed…under a dilemma which I cannot solve but by an exposition of the naked truth," Jefferson went on to admit that he had in fact penned the Resolutions and that "he would have wished this rather to have remained as hitherto, without inquiry, but your inquiries have a right to be answered."[59]

The deep connections between the Breckinridge family and Thomas Jefferson continued practically up to the time of Jefferson's death in 1826. James Breckinridge, John's brother, a close associate of Jefferson's for decades, continued to practice law in Virginia in the early 1800s and served with distinction in the War of 1812. At the request of Jefferson, James Breckinridge was one of the original founders of the University of Virginia. An interesting letter from Jefferson to Breckinridge in 1818 refers to Jefferson's trip back to Monticello after meeting with him and others on the founding of this university.

Evidently, Jefferson, then seventy-eight, had fallen ill, and he wrote to Breckinridge about the hardship of traveling by horse carriage over the "rocks and mountains" of rural Virginia. Later in 1825, James Breckinridge, then sixty-two, again exchanged correspondence with Jefferson, eighty-six, on three occasions.

By this time, John Breckinridge had long since died in 1806. But the legacy of his son, his family down through the ages and even his brother up to the time of Jefferson's death is an unmistakable bond of friendship and shared political history. These connections not only produced the controversial Kentucky Resolutions but also created the opportunity for inclusion in Kentucky's constitution of the strong separation of powers provisions that Jefferson favored and which left a legacy of progress for Kentucky.

Jefferson's connections if not his intellectual interest in Kentucky did not end with the death of John Breckinridge or his correspondence with others in the Breckinridge family. Although Jefferson was never recorded as visiting the state, he had a close association with explorer William Clark, who had a home in Louisville, Kentucky, through 1803. When he was president, Jefferson commissioned Clark to head up the famous expedition with Meriwether Lewis, designed in part to explore the nation's new territory following the Louisiana Purchase.

In the months leading up to the start of the expedition, Jefferson corresponded with them, urging both to be on the lookout for unknown animal species and, incredibly, urged them to search for evidence of prehistoric mastodons on the trip. Meriwether Lewis understood that mastodon bones might indeed be found at Big Bone Lick in Northern Kentucky. As late as 1807, Jefferson was writing to Clark on this subject and ultimately dispatched him to Big Bone Lick to obtain fossilized mastodon bones, which were shipped to Jefferson personally. To this day, Jefferson's home in Virginia, Monticello, preserves several relics forwarded to him from the Lewis and Clark Expedition.[60]

A final connection of Jefferson to Kentucky that forms an intersection with John Breckinridge was Jefferson's long-standing friendship with John Brown. Brown is commonly referred to as the "Father of Kentucky," for while a member of Congress from Virginia, he introduced in 1792 the bill granting statehood to Kentucky. Brown, like John Breckinridge, studied law at the College of William & Mary and served as a member of Congress from Virginia from 1789 through 1792. The two men were also apparently cousins, with their mothers having the maiden name "Preston," and Brown was born near Staunton, Virginia, as was Breckinridge.

Undoubtedly, Brown interacted with Breckinridge, and when he moved to Kentucky, he established a fine residence on Wilkinson Street in what is now the historic district of Frankfort, Kentucky's capital. Brown was closely involved along with Breckinridge in Kentucky's political and constitutional affairs, and when Kentucky's legislature elected Brown to the U.S. Senate, he was one of only four senators in that body to vote against the use of military force in the Quasi-War with France, reflecting his state's affinity to the French nation and opposition to the Alien and Sedition Acts.

The Breckinridge legacy has continued through our nation's history. John's two sons were pioneer leaders of Kentucky. Joseph served in the Kentucky General Assembly and as Speaker of the state House in 1818; Robert, a Presbyterian minister, served in the state House as well. Of all the family, the most notable was John Cabell Breckinridge (1821–1875), grandson of Jefferson's colleague, who was vice president of the United States. Serving from 1857 to 1861 under President James Buchanan, he remains the youngest person (at age thirty-six) ever elected that office. (Interestingly, almost a century later, another Kentuckian, Alben Barkley, was the oldest person ever elected to serve as vice president.)

John C. Breckinridge, who also served in the Kentucky House and in Congress prior to 1857, was an unsuccessful candidate for president against Abraham Lincoln in 1860. A Confederate partisan, this Breckinridge was elected to the U.S. Senate in 1859, and he served there briefly—from the end of his vice presidency until his resignation in 1861 to become a Confederate general.

Breckinridge served with distinction and remarkably survived some of the most difficult battles of the war, including Shiloh, Cold Harbor and much of the Wilderness Campaign. After the war, he exiled first in Paris, next in Great Britain and then returned to the United States, arriving in Lexington in 1869 after President Andrew Johnson proclaimed amnesty the previous year for all former Confederate soldiers. In 1875, he died in the same city where he was born, Lexington, Kentucky, at the relatively young age of fifty-four after a life of constant activity.

Other members of the Breckinridge family continued to choose public service as a career, many of them serving as ambassadors, members of Kentucky's General Assembly and even as a member of Congress and Kentucky attorney general, as did John Bayne Breckinridge (1973–79)—exactly as his ancestor John Breckinridge had done when he was Kentucky's attorney general nearly two hundred years before in 1793.[61]

Thomas Jefferson to James Breckinridge
Monticello Oct. 6. 18.

Dear Sir

You have had a right to suppose me very unmindful of my promise to furnish you with drawings for your Courthouse. yet the fact is not so. a few days after I parted with you, the use of the waters of the warm spring began to affect me sensibly & unfavorably, and at length produced serious imposthume & eruption, with fever, colliquative sweats, & extreme debility. these sufferings aggravated by the torment of the journey home, over the rocks and mountains I had to pass, had reduced me to the lowest stage of exhaustion by the time I had got back. I have been on the recovery some time and still am so: but not yet able to sit erect for writing. by working at your drawings a little every day, I have been able to complete, & now to forward them by mail. with the explanations accompanying them, I hope your workman will sufficiently understand them. I send also some seed of the Succory which I think I promised you.

I cannot omit this occasion of acknowledging to you my sensibility for your kind attentions on our journey, and during our stay together at the springs. long kept by other vocations from an every-day intercourse with the world, I feel the need of a Mentor, when I enter it, & especially in an unknown society: and I found the benefit of it in your kind cares. I only lament that the knowledge of your worth and goodness comes to me when so little of life remains to cultivate and to merit it's cordial reciprocation. if my health should become again as firm as it was before the unlucky experiment of the springs, I shall not despair in my annual rambles to the Natural Bridge, of being able at some time to extend them to Fincastle, towards which the pleasure of visiting you would be the chief inducement. nor will I despair that some of your journeyings, on private or public account, may lead you thro' our quarter, and give me the gratification of seeing you at Monticello. with deep & permanent impressions of cordial esteem, accept the assurance of my affectionate attachment and high respect.

Th. Jefferson[62]

Chapter 8

JEFFERSON AND KENTUCKY'S CONSTITUTION

Why the Balance of Power Provisions Were Not Included in Our Federal Constitution

Excepting Virginia, the Kentucky Resolutions were not adopted in other state legislatures, although they were delivered from Jefferson to John Breckinridge, adopted by the Kentucky General Assembly and served as a vehicle for local outrage in Central Kentucky. It was this same energy from Jefferson that fed into the separation of powers clauses critical to the history of Kentucky that most likely had been proposed by Jefferson and survive to this day in our state constitution.

These are the very provisions of the state's constitution cited in the quote at the outset of this book from an 1898 opinion of Kentucky's Supreme Court and supported through the landmark opinion of the Kentucky Supreme Court in *LRC v. Brown* and its progeny of cases. These opinions in 1898, 1922, 1984 and 2004 reference in varying degrees the history of how Kentuckians in their writing of the Kentucky Constitution in 1792 received these sections from Jefferson, which continue to add meaning to our everyday lives. These provisions were maintained at the 1799 Kentucky Constitutional Convention, at which Breckinridge played a leading role. They are worth quoting in full as they now exist in the Kentucky Constitution:

> *Section 27.* ***Powers of Government divided among legislative, executive, and judicial departments.*** *The powers of the government of the Commonwealth of Kentucky shall be divided into three distinct departments, and each of them be confined to a separate body of magistracy, to wit: Those which are legislative, to one; those which are executive, to another; and those which are judicial, to another.*

Section 28. **One department not to exercise power belonging to another.** *No person or collection of persons, being of one of those departments, shall exercise any power properly belonging to either of the others, except in the instances hereinafter expressly directed or permitted.*[63]

Seemingly innocuous, these provisions play a critical role in the balance of power among the three branches of government in Kentucky and repeatedly have been used to advance critical policy decisions. Over and over, they have been deployed in case law, countless memoranda and even political instances to justify or refute a great policy initiative, as we shall see. More importantly, the Kentucky Supreme Court repeatedly pointed to these sections as limiting the power of the General Assembly in overreaching its authority, or they were offered as support to curb the perceived power of a particular governor or even the judiciary.

In a 1984 *Kentucky Law Journal* article, "The Separation of Governmental Powers Under the Constitution of Kentucky: A Legal and Historical Analysis of *LRC v. Brown*,"[64] constitutional scholar and attorney Sheryl G. Snyder and University of Kentucky historian Robert M. Ireland stated (emphasis added):

> **The provision expressly incorporating the doctrine of separation of governmental powers into Kentucky's Constitution was drafted by Thomas Jefferson, and composed the first two paragraphs of Kentucky's first, second and third Constitutions.** *Jefferson's words appear in the present Constitution of Kentucky immediately after the Bill of Rights and form "an unusually forceful" Separation of Powers Clause.*

Kentucky was not the first state for which Jefferson may have proposed an explicit separation of powers provision in a state constitution; he had done an identical thing in his 1783 *Draft of a Constitution for Virginia.* In this draft, Jefferson included a simple but forceful directive:

> *The legislative, executive and judiciary departments shall be separate and distinct so that no person, or collection of persons of any of them shall exercise any power properly belonging to either of the others, except in the instances here and after expressly permitted.*[65]

In addition to what is suggested in the balance of this chapter, Jefferson's passion for separation of powers was demonstrated in rather forceful language in his *Notes on the State of Virginia* (1781). Calling concentration of power in the hands of one of three branches of government "precisely the definition of despotic government," Jefferson singled out as noteworthy an action of the first convention on Virginia's constitution. We may recall that George Nicholas in his notes for the 1792 Kentucky Constitutional Convention referenced page 195 from the 1787 London edition of Jefferson's *Notes on the State of Virginia*. On this page, Jefferson wrote of separations of powers (emphasis added):

> *For this reason that convention, which passed the ordinance of government,* **laid its foundation on this basis, that the legislative, executive and judiciary departments should be separate and distinct so that no person should exercise the powers of more than one of them at the same time.** *But no barrier was provided between these several powers. The judiciary and executive members were left dependent on the legislative, for their subsistence in office and some of them for their continuance in it. If therefore the legislature assumes the executive and judiciary powers, no opposition is likely to be made nor if made can it be effectual because in that case, they may put their proceedings into the form of an act of assembly which will render them obligatory on the other branches.*[66]

Ultimately, and as a window into what Jefferson likely had in store for Kentucky, the Virginia Constitution contained a distinctly similar version of Jefferson's initial proposal. To this day, Virginia's constitution contains the following provision, which Jefferson likely constructed:

> *Article III Division of Powers*
> *Section 1. Departments to be Distinct.*
>
> *The legislative, executive, and judicial departments shall be separate and distinct, so that none exercise the powers properly belonging to the others, nor any person exercise the power of more than one of them at the same time; Provided, however, administrative agencies may be created by the General Assembly with such authority and duties as the General Assembly may be prescribe....*

To be fair, Jefferson's probable work with the constitutions of Virginia and Kentucky is not among the only example of states admitted to the Union relatively early that had distinct separation of powers provisions.

Although there is no record of Jefferson being involved in development of the Massachusetts Constitution and its Bill of Rights in 1780, it is likely that John Adams heavily influenced that document. When contrasting the Virginia and Kentucky provisions, Massachusetts went much further in its directive for a distinct separation of the branches of government. The 1780 Massachusetts Declaration of Rights stated:

> *In the government of this Commonwealth, the legislative department shall never exercise the executive and judicial power, or either of them: the executive shall never exercise the legislative and judicial powers or either of them: the judicial shall never exercise the legislative and executive powers, or either of them: to the end it may be a government of laws and not of men.*[67]

Jefferson's near obsession with including a separation of powers provision in Virginia's constitution and perhaps Kentucky's is evidenced by the fact that Jefferson may have tried but failed to include this provision in the U.S. Constitution. History tells us that Madison, John Jay and others were the principal authors of this document but declined to include such provisions proposed by Jefferson. An interesting account of this dilemma can be found in *The Federalist Papers*, authored anonymously by Madison, Jay and Alexander Hamilton in 1787 and 1788. Here, Hamilton and Jay presented, and Madison opposed, Jefferson's unsuccessful proposal for a separation of powers clause in our federal Constitution.[68]

This is worthy of discussion because it can be inferred that Jefferson's frustration with not including separation of powers provisions within the federal Constitution perhaps fueled his passion to include them, when he was consulted, in the constitutions of Virginia and Kentucky. A good deal of Jefferson's sentiments in this regard may very well stem from his anti-royalist tendencies and deep suspicion of the British constitution.[69] Even Madison, in his *Federalist* no. 47 essay, remarked on the structure of our new government and the distribution of power among its different parts, opposing the inclusion of a separation of powers clause in the federal Constitution. In this essay, he reflected on the strong sentiment of the founding fathers against the British constitution, and as a principal author of our federal Constitution, Madison stated his strong concern with the British construct when he said:

> [W]*e must perceive that the legislative, executive, and judiciary departments are by no means totally separate and distinct from each other. The executive magistrate forms an integral part of the legislative authority, he alone has*

the prerogative of making treaties with foreign sovereigns which, when made, have under certain limitations the force of legislative acts. All the members of the judiciary department are appointed by him can be removed by him on the address of the two Houses of Parliament and form, when he pleases to consult them, one of his constitutional councils. One branch of the legislative department forms also a great constitutional council to the executive chief, as, on the other hand, it is the sole depository of judicial power in cases of impeachment and is invested with the supreme appellate jurisdiction in all other cases. The judges, again, are so far connected with the legislative department as often to attend and participate in its deliberations though not admitted to a legislative vote.[70]

In this *Federalist* essay, he then quoted Montesquieu, the eighteenth-century French philosopher known as the primary source of the theory of separation of governmental powers: "There can be no liberty where the legislative and executive powers are united in the same person, or body of magistrates."[71] Despite Madison's and Jefferson's shared concern about the concentration of power in the British political structure, it's remarkable the lengths to which Madison went in *Federalist* essays no. 47 and no. 48 to refute the need for the type of separation of powers clause ultimately included in Kentucky's constitution.

In meticulous detail, Madison reviewed the constitution of several states—South Carolina, Georgia and North Carolina and others—making the argument that there is naturally an intersection of powers among the branches of government. He went on to suggest that in some states, the executive department was filled by appointments of the legislature, while in others, justices of the peace, a judiciary office, were appointed by the legislature. He then pointed out that in some states the executive in the case of a governor has the prerogative of pardon and commutation of sentences for criminal convictions, which is explored later in this book. Even the judiciary was mentioned by Madison as technically sharing one of its powers in some state constitutions, providing the legislature can sit as a jury for impeachment trials.

Finally, in the concluding essay on this topic (no. 48), Madison mentioned, albeit respectfully, the target of his concern: Jefferson himself. In doing so, Madison stated by way of example (emphasis added):

That of Virginia, a state which, as we have seen, has expressly declared in its constitution that the three great departments ought not to be intermixed.

The authority in support of it is Mr. Jefferson, who, besides his other advantages for remaking the operation of the government, was himself the chief magistrate of it. In order to convey fully the ideas with which his experience has impressed upon him on this subject it will be necessary to quote a passage of some length from his very interesting Notes on the State of Virginia. "All the powers of government, legislative, executive, and judiciary result to the legislative body. The concentrating of these in the same hands is precisely the definition of despotic government."[72]

Essentially, Madison was making the argument that Jefferson's demand for a separation of powers provision in the federal Constitution and its inclusion in state constitutions was an overreaction. Jefferson, as we have seen and will see in coming chapters, was not deterred in supporting separation of powers clauses in state constitutions such as Kentucky's, which have been quoted through the years in court opinions, validating some of Kentucky's greatest reforms. At the time, however, Madison was not persuaded and, in the final sentence of his *Federalist* no. 48 essay, stated (emphasis added):

The conclusion which I am warranted in drawing from these observations is that **a mere demarcation on parchment of the constitutional limits of the several departments is not a sufficient guard against those encroachments which lead to a tyrannical concentration of all the powers of Government in the same hands.**[73]

Another reason Jefferson may have failed to place a separation of powers provision in the federal Constitution is his fractious relationship with President John Adams, with whom he served as vice president. Adams was among the strongest advocates for independence at the Second Continental Congress in the summer of 1776. While he ceded much of the writing of the Declaration of Independence to Thomas Jefferson, he was involved later along with Madison, John Jay and others in the structure of the federal Constitution in 1787.

Although Adams was overseas serving as minister to the United Kingdom in 1787, as was Jefferson as minister to France, Adams was an active participant remotely and published that year his treatise calling for balanced government titled "Defense of the Constitutions of Government of the United States of America."[74] Adams, however, seemed to have a contrarian personality and was often viewed by his colleagues as being rude, highly opinionated and impetuous. He even complained in a letter to his wife that he was himself "obnoxious, suspected and unpopular."

Jefferson, from all accounts, was a last-minute addition to Congress when the Declaration of Independence was written mostly by himself. He was elected as a replacement for his mother's cousin and was somewhat unknown when he arrived in Philadelphia in 1776. He was the opposite physically and by personality of Adams—stood tall and erect, was freckled and had bright-red hair.[75] He was viewed as modest and unassuming, soft-spoken with a high-pitched voice. He worked diligently and basically on his own as the principal author of the Declaration of Independence. In 1790, William Maclay, a U.S. senator from Pennsylvania, after meeting with Jefferson, said that he "is a slender man; has rather the air of stiffness in his manner; his clothes seem too small for him; he sits in a lounging manner, on one hip commonly and with one of his shoulders elevated much above the other; his face has a sunny aspect; his whole figure has a loose shackling air."[76]

These two men continued to circle each other as political adversaries and, as previously detailed, came to lead the two main political parties of the time, with Adams as leader of the Federalists and Jefferson as leader of the Democratic-Republicans. An interesting account of how King George III of the United Kingdom viewed these two men is contained in Andrew Jackson O'Shaughnessy's brilliant book *The Men Who Lost America: British Leadership, the American Revolution and the Fate of the Empire*. In compelling detail, O'Shaughnessy wrote of the brief but cordial meeting Adams had in 1795 with the king at St. James's Palace in London. Adams "was delighted that his person, his status, and his country had been accorded respect and kindness beyond his expectations from the King. Adams and his wife Abigail subsequently became quite fond of George III."[77]

Adams likewise later reported that the king "made the three reverences" or acknowledgments to Adams upon being shown into his chambers—"one at the door, another about halfway, and the third before the presence, according to the usual establishment at this and all the northern courts of Europe." Adams went on to report that when the king jokingly suggested Adams was "not the most attached of all your countrymen to the manners of France," Adams replied, "I have no attachment but to my own country," to which the king simply replied, "An honest man will never have any other."[78] The next year, in 1786, Adams, serving as first minister of the United States to the United Kingdom, organized an audience for Jefferson and himself with George III. O'Shaughnessy's book relates that from Jefferson's perspective, this meeting did not go well at all. Thirty-five years later, in his autobiography, Jefferson recalled the event and stated that "it was impossible for anything to be more ungracious" than the notice that George III gave "Mr. Adams and myself."[79]

Jefferson's resentment of King George was long-standing, and it remains notable in the Declaration of Independence, where he wrote in detail of the king's everyday oppression of colonial affairs. In this document, he said that the King was "[a] prince whose character is marked by every act which may define a tyrant" and "unfit to be the ruler of a free people."[80] This may be seen as yet another indication of Jefferson's determination to include a separation of powers provision in the constitutions of states such as Kentucky, when he could not place one in the federal Constitution, because he feared the concentration of power in any one branch of government.

The relationship between Jefferson and Adams was a roller coaster if there ever was one. Bonded despite differences at Philadelphia in 1776, their friendship deepened while on diplomatic missions to Europe serving as ministers to France and the United Kingdom. On one occasion, while both men served overseas, Jefferson visited Adams and joined him on a trip to Stratford-upon-Avon, the childhood home of William Shakespeare. Jefferson recorded that both men followed a time-honored custom by cutting off a piece of wood as a souvenir from a chair in which Shakespeare supposedly sat. This friendship temporarily fractured in the late 1790s over the Alien and Sedition Acts and then in 1800 in the contentious presidential race. In time, as the two aged, they would renew their friendship in a historic exchange of correspondence that continued until their deaths in 1826.

Adams demonstrated that he was still capable of being acerbic with Jefferson when he wrote to him in a July 1813 letter, for example: "Your administration will be quoted by philosophers as a model of profound wisdom; by politicians as weak, superficial and short sighted." Jefferson, however, took it all in good stride, having long since become accustomed to Adams's bluntness. One of Jefferson's last letters to John Adams, on March 25, 1826, was to ask

John Adams, president of the United States, 1797–1801. Portrait by John Trumbull, 1793. *National Portrait Gallery, Washington, D.C.*

Adams if he might visit with his grandson, Thomas Jefferson Randolph, on a trip he was making to Boston. Both men died on the fiftieth anniversary of the signing of the Declaration of Independence on July 4, 1826.[81]

As a practical matter, most Kentuckians, and even the leadership of the state through the nineteenth century and into the early twentieth century, had little idea of the relevance of these constitutional provisions influenced by Jefferson. And in any event, given what little was recognized, most politicians assumed that everything was settled law and had been hashed out by the courts or the legislature on these matters for decades. This could not have been further from the truth. By the early twentieth century, Kentucky found itself in the middle of a series of constitutional struggles involving all three branches of government. But first some interesting historical context should be given before describing the modern-day trial by fire of Kentucky's constitution and how its interpretation put Kentucky on a path to greater prosperity.

Chapter 9

THE KENTUCKY SUPREME COURT WEIGHS IN ON THE STATE CONSTITUTION AND ASSERTS JEFFERSON WROTE PORTIONS OF IT

In 1821, at the age of seventy-seven, Jefferson wrote a document of more than two hundred pages commonly referred to as his autobiography but which Jefferson himself referred to as "some memoranda and recollections of dates and facts concerning myself," largely written for "ready reference and for the information of my family." This writing is notable for several revelations, including the tracing of his family lineage to Wales in the United Kingdom and the unusual length to which he wrote with affection for the legal instruction he received in Virginia from George Wythe, who "continued to be my faithful and beloved mentor in youth and my most affectionate friend through life." Wythe, as previously mentioned, also mentored John Breckinridge and Henry Clay.[82]

He goes on in other places to relate the rather turgid experience he had "on my presentation as usual to the king and queen at their levies" and his view as to the less-than-gracious way in which the king chose to address him on these occasions. He did not capitalize the first letters of *king* and *queen* in the original writing of this recollection. But perhaps the most interesting portions of the autobiography for our purposes are the great lengths to which he goes in this document to emphasize the need for the independence of the various branches of government—judicial, legislative and executive.[83]

Great portions of his writing relate his criticism of the efforts at constitutional reform in France during his tenure as minister to that country and detail criticism of the structure of the British government for placing unusual power in the executive, which in both countries was a king.

He seemed appalled that English judges were appointed at the pleasure of the Crown, later revised to last "during good behavior." He considered as weak a judiciary that was completely "dependent on the will of the king which had proved itself the most oppressive of all tools in the hands of that magistrate."[84]

A little over sixty years after Jefferson wrote these words, first in 1898 and next in 1922, the highest court of Kentucky, then known as the Court of Appeals, more than exercised its judicial independence as a separate branch of government in applying Jefferson's separation of powers provisions in landmark decisions. The landmark decision *Sibert v. Garrett* is perhaps more notable for its direct reliance on Jefferson's work. This was a blockbuster case at the time that considered and then traced the history and modern-day application of Jefferson's separation of powers provisions as contained in Kentucky's constitution under Sections 27 and 28. More importantly, the Court's decision relied heavily on these sections of the constitution in its final ruling.[85]

The *Sibert* case concerned the constitutionality of a bill attempted to be passed by the General Assembly that would have empowered the legislature, as opposed to the governor, to appoint the members of the State Highway Commission. At this time and for a great portion of the twentieth century, this powerful commission was responsible for the construction of critical roadways, most of which were badly needed in rural areas. The constitutionality of this proposed act was quickly attacked on grounds that the legislature possessed "no constitutional right to name in the bill the first members of the Commission or to elect their successors thereafter."[86]

In what for its time was an exceptionally lengthy opinion, the Court deemed the construction of the bill to be unconstitutional, but in doing so, it relied heavily on the separation of powers provisions in Kentucky's constitution, the very provisions Jefferson favored. In finding this state law to be violative of Kentucky's constitution, the Court found that the legislature had unlawfully and unconstitutionally encroached on the powers of a separate branch of government to make such appointments, that being the governor in the form of the executive branch.

This appears to be the second case in which the Court of Appeals traced in detail the unique constitutional history of Kentucky, which included these provisions attributed to Jefferson. The first case was the 1898 decision *Commissioners of Sinking Fund v. George*. This case upheld the constitutionality of legislation empowering the General Assembly to appoint members of an administrative body when no related statute or constitutional provision otherwise forbade it. While lengthy, it is relevant to our story to quote portions of the Court's opinion in both cases, which trace the alleged involvement of Jefferson, with George Nicholas and John Breckinridge, in developing Kentucky's constitution (emphasis added):

> *When Mr. Jefferson returned from France, the federal constitution had been adopted; and…he obtained permission to go to Monticello for some months. John Breckinridge and George Nicholas paid him a visit there and informed him that Kentucky was about to frame a constitution for herself, and that Virginia was about to permit Kentucky to become a separate and independent state.* **He told them there was danger in the federal constitution because the clause defining the powers of the departments of government was not sufficiently guarded and that the first thing to be provided for by the Kentucky constitution should be to confine the judiciary to its powers and the legislative and executive to theirs. Mr. Jefferson drew the form of the provision and gave it to Nicholas and Breckinridge; And it was taken by Nicholas to the convention which met at Danville and there presented it—Breckinridge not being present at the convention.** *There was much discussion and dissent when the article was offered, but, when its author was made known, the respect of Kentucky for the great name of Jefferson carried it through and it was at once adopted.*

Justice George DuRelle of the Kentucky Supreme Court (then called the Kentucky Court of Appeals) dissented in the Court's decision *Commissioners of Sinking Fund v. George* (1898).[87]

Twenty-two years later, in the *Sibert* decision, the Court again referenced in detail its view as to the work of Jefferson on Kentucky's constitution when it stated in pertinent part (emphasis added):

> *Perhaps no state forming a part of the national government of the United States has a constitution whose language more emphatically separates and perpetuates what might be termed the American tripod form of government, then does our (Kentucky) constitution,* **which history tells us came from the pen of the great declaimer of American independence, Thomas Jefferson, when delegates from Kentucky, just after it was admitted to the union, waited upon him and he penned for them the substance of what is now Section 28, supra, of our constitution, containing an affirmative prohibition against**

one department exercising powers properly belonging to the others and which without it contained only the negative prohibition found in Section 27 of that instrument and which was the extent of the separation of the powers found in the federal constitution and in those of a number of the states composing the confederated union at the time.

Following the adoption of our first constitution, other incoming states, either in their first constitutions or in subsequent ones, copied, either literally or in substance, the two sections of our constitution and the courts of some of them have announced divergent views as to the proper construction of the two sections, and in nearly every instance the opinion was made to turn upon the existence of some fact or facts extraneous to their language, notably among which were other provisions of the constitution containing them, and which were made to apply to the particular facts under consideration and thereby furnish the reason for the particular conclusion reached.[88]

This was particularly strong language extoling the heritage of Kentucky's constitution in relation to Jefferson's work on it. It is notable that the Court in the second excerpt in the *Sibert* case emphasized this lineage one hundred years ago from our present day and one hundred years after Jefferson, in his old age, was justifying the need for independence among the branches of government. While the Court in the *Sibert* case held that the Kentucky legislature had exceeded its power, which Jefferson's separation of powers provisions were designed to prevent, the Court did not stop here. It doubled down on its reasoning and expanded on the critical advantages to the independence in operation of our three branches of government. To further quote the Court in the *Sibert* opinion (emphasis added):

It cannot fail to be observed that the reasons underlying the separation of our republican form of government into the three branches was to prevent one of the departments from absorbing and appropriating unto itself the functions of either of the others. The purpose was to have each of them to so operate in their respective spheres as to create checks to the operations of the others and to prevent the formation by one department of an oligarchy through the absorption of powers belonging to the others; the evil effects from such concentration of powers were outstanding in the pages of past history the instances of which we need not stop to enumerate.

It was to prevent such evil effects and a possible eventual revolution, and to preserve and forever perpetuate, if possible,

the constitutional form of government, that sections 27 and 28
of the Kentucky constitution and similar ones were adopted.

In a final tip of the hat to Jefferson, the Court went on to state that it had an affirmative duty "to pronounce an act unconstitutional when it's enactment is either expressly or by necessary implication inhibited and subversive of the purposes and intention of the makers of the particular Constitution under consideration."[89]

Even though these decisions were handed down long ago, it is lost in history as to whether the courts that made them had any inkling as to the extent their language would be quoted for generations to come. As we shall see, this lengthy discourse on Kentucky's separation of powers provisions, its unique implications and the notion they may have been provided to Kentucky by Jefferson were deciding factors in future decisions as to the constitutionality of some of Kentucky's greatest reforms.

Chapter 10

THE KENTUCKY SUPREME COURT, CHIEF JUSTICE STEPHENS AND HIS USE OF JEFFERSON'S PROVISIONS TO REMAKE KENTUCKY

While the bulk of public policy relates to reforms principally initiated by the executive and legislative branches, the coequal branch of the judiciary at the federal and state level played a critical role in Kentucky, advancing landmark reforms for the public good. Kentucky is fortunate to have had Nicholas, Breckinridge and likely Jefferson involved in developing key portions of Kentucky's constitution that explicitly emphasize the coequal nature of the executive, legislative and judicial branches. Governors of Kentucky took seriously their role in relation to the judiciary, in particular the appointment of judges to fill temporary vacancies in the lower courts and among appellate courts, including the Kentucky Supreme Court, as the highest state tribunal came to be called in the late 1970s.

Governors have the laborious task of working on judicial appointments in the case of a vacancy and interviewing the candidates, most of whom have sponsors and associates who pepper a governor's office with calls and letters of support. Governors in the late twentieth century played a crucial role in judicial appointments across the state and grew to recognize one person whom they could rely on confidentially to guide them in this process. This person was Robert Stephens (1927–2002), who served as chief justice of the Kentucky Supreme Court for more than twenty years.

Remarkably, Stephens went on after his resignation from the Court as chief justice to serve in the Patton administration as justice secretary, being appointed to this position in 1999 at the age of seventy-one. Once he took the job, he was a trusted advisor to the governor and the administration on a variety of matters and threw himself into his role with a whirlwind tour of judicial outposts around the state, including the state prison system. For our purposes, however, the contributions of Stephens as a keen interpreter of Kentucky's constitution and his application of the principles of separation of powers as likely set forth by Jefferson cannot be underestimated. Repeatedly, Stephens applied provisions of the constitution over his twenty-year tenure on the Court to materially advance Kentucky in the fields of education, tax reform, job creation and the structure of government itself.

In the world of many, Stephens was legendary in the legal and political community. Countless lawyers remember vividly being sworn in as a new lawyer by Stephens in the Supreme Court chambers and were humbled at the time after the ceremony he usually spent with a new lawyer and their family. Stephens once described himself as an "aging idealist," but when Governor Paul Patton posthumously dedicated the new Fayette County Courthouse in the chief justice's honor in 2002, he said that Stephens was "the most influential political figure in Kentucky in the 20th Century."[90]

In a career that spanned more than thirty years of public service, Stephens either personally crafted or was closely associated with resolution of the major legal and public policy issues of our day. He was the longest-serving chief justice in the modern history of the Kentucky Supreme Court and the third-longest-serving in the nation. Previously as Fayette County judge, he was an architect of merged government in the Bluegrass long before Louisville and Jefferson County merged their governmental systems. Stephens tirelessly supported this reform in Fayette County when he knew, in the 1970s, that it would eliminate his job as county judge.

As a Supreme Court justice, the historic decision on education reform that he wrote in 1989, may be his most notable legacy. This decision is on the same level, arguably, as *LRC (Legislative Research Commission) v. Brown* and the landmark Toyota decision (to be discussed shortly), which opened a new era of job creation throughout Kentucky. The decision on education struck down the unequal funding of public schools and led the legislature to approve the landmark Kentucky Education Reform Act (1991) under Governor Wallace Wilkinson. This reform set Kentucky on the path to dramatically improve the educational system for thousands of children, particularly in rural areas, which may have been treated at least fiscally on an unequal basis.[91]

In the 1989 school funding decision declaring Kentucky's public school system unconstitutional (*Rose v. Council for Better Education*), Stephens deployed skillfully and with stunning precision the separation of powers provisions

Jefferson allegedly wrote for Kentucky's constitution, and he noted in the opinion that Jefferson did so. The summary of the Stephens holding from June 8, 1989, is worth repeating here and is followed by the portion of the ruling where he recognized Jefferson's authorship of these provisions and their applicability to this case. In this instance, the opinion said that the judiciary was well within its constitutional bounds to declare the school system unconstitutional, paving the way for historic education reform:

> *The issue we decide on this appeal is whether the Kentucky General Assembly has complied with its constitutional mandate to "provide an efficient system of common schools throughout the state." In deciding that it has not, we intend no criticism of the substantial efforts made by the present General Assembly and by its predecessors, nor do we intend to substitute our judicial authority for the authority and discretion of the General Assembly. We are, rather, exercising our constitutional duty in declaring that, when we consider the evidence in the record, and when we apply the constitutional requirement of Section 183 to that evidence, it is crystal clear that the General Assembly has fallen short of its duty to enact legislation to provide for an efficient system of common schools throughout the state. In a word, the present system of common schools in Kentucky is not an "efficient" one in our view of the clear mandate of Section 183. The common school system in Kentucky is constitutionally deficient.*[92]

While this quoted section of the decision on the state's educational system constituted a summary of the ruling, Stephens did not hesitate to bring Jefferson's contribution to Kentucky's constitution alive in rather bold language. Building on his previous work in the decision *LRC v. Brown*, Stephens recognized specifically the contributions of Jefferson to our state constitution. In doing this, he used these provisions to defeat the argument that the judiciary was infringing on the powers of a separate branch of government, that being the legislative body. In the Court's decision, Stephens stated (emphasis added):

> *XII. Did the Trial Court's Judgment Violate the Separation of Powers Provision of the Kentucky Constitution?*
>
> *Appellants assert that the trial court's judgment violates the separation of powers doctrine in that it exceeded the authority of the court in "dictating" to the General Assembly, and it exceeded the authority of the*

court by creating a type of open-ended judgment which required legislator-defendants to report their progress to the trial court. **Our constitutional provisions which relate to separation of powers between the three separate and independent branches of government were authored by Thomas Jefferson. They are as follows:**

"Sec. 27. The powers of the government of the Commonwealth of Kentucky shall be divided into three distinct departments, and each of them be confined to a separate body of the magistracy, to-wit: Those which are legislative, to one; those which are executive, to another; and those which are judicial, to another."

"Sec. 28. No person or collection of persons, being of one of those departments, shall exercise any power properly belonging to either of the others, except in the instances hereinafter expressly directed or permitted."

Section 29 vests the legislative power in the General Assembly, and Section 109 grants the judicial power to the Court of Justice.

Because of the specific wording of the Constitution, we have previously noted the strength of the separation of powers doctrine in this state:

"Our present Constitution contains explicit provisions which, on one hand, mandate separation among the three branches of government, and on the other hand, specifically prohibit incursion of one branch of government into the powers and functions of the other. Thus, our constitution has a double-barreled, positive-negative approach...." *Legislative Research Commission v. Brown, Ky., 664 S.W.2d 907, 912 (1984). Moreover, in Brown, we reiterated that the doctrine of separation of powers must be "strictly construed." Id.*

Simply stated, we have declared that the power to legislate belongs to the General Assembly, and the power to adjudicate belongs to the judiciary. It is our goal to honor both the letter and spirit of that constitutional mandate.[93]

Chief Justice Stephens could not have been more explicit in his recognition of Thomas Jefferson's impact on Kentucky's constitution. Many lawyers and others in the Lexington area still remember visiting the law school library in the 1980s and seeing Stephens sitting alone at a table, with his reading glasses down over his nose, several yellow legal pads in front of him on which he was working and stacks of law books and case decisions spread around him. He was not only a great student of the law, but he was also a student of history and chose over and over in his opinions to state with apparent pride the unique nature of Kentucky's constitution and Jefferson's contribution to it.

Further, Stephens's prior opinion in *LRC v. Brown* in 1984 remains the benchmark of constitutional scholarship and the delicate balance of power among our three branches of state government. This decision was wide-ranging and fought back an effort by the Kentucky General Assembly, acting through its Legislative Research Commission in the interim between legislative sessions, to assume what the Court ruled were executive functions in making certain appointments and otherwise encroaching on the powers of the executive branch. Highly regarded constitutional scholar and Louisville attorney Sheryl Snyder, who represented Governor John Y. Brown Jr. in that case before the Kentucky Supreme Court, fittingly called the decision Kentucky's equivalent of *Marbury v. Madison* (1803). In doing so, he called forth U.S. Chief Justice John Marshall's landmark opinion upholding the principle of judicial review.[94]

Thanks to the lawyering of Snyder and others, the Kentucky Supreme Court was persuaded, as it had done before and would do again, to deploy Jefferson's separation of power provisions in Kentucky's constitution as they may very well have been intended. Just as we saw in the *Sibert* decision in 1922, which was quoted in Chief Justice Stephens's opinion in *LRC v. Brown*, Sections 27 and 28 of Kentucky's constitution protecting the distinct powers of each branch of government were used to defeat the legislative encroachment on the powers of the executive branch. In this case, the General Assembly had essentially exercised a veto over executive actions by the governor between legislative sessions.

The 1803 decision in *Marbury* established the authority of the federal judiciary to determine the constitutionality of legislative enactments, just as *LRC v. Brown* in Kentucky drew stark lines of limitations of the respective powers of the executive and legislative branches. Lawyers in state government for decades have consulted the *LRC v. Brown* opinion, particularly when they were challenged by the General Assembly passing legislation viewed as infringing on the power of the executive to implement laws, as is the constitutional duty of the executive, through administrative regulations and executive orders.[95]

Chief Justice Stephens was also known as an innovator in the administration of Kentucky's court system, and he used political skills honed in Lexington politics to achieve his goals. From the outset of his tenure on the Court, Stephens was determined to give meaning to the due process clause of the state constitution by equipping Kentucky courtrooms with state-of-the-art video technology. That is a reform the federal judiciary, including the U.S. Supreme Court, should perhaps consider today. This technology served as the actual court record of a case, replacing the time-consuming transcription process of court reporting as the sole record. Court reporters initially opposed the reform, but their attitudes changed and their business remained brisk. Stephens took other steps with computers to further cut the delay of justice, bringing Kentucky courts closer to a paperless system that has advanced even beyond his vision to the largely electronic system we have today.

Likewise, Stephens's role in two cases that advanced economic development in Kentucky is widely heralded in the state and elsewhere. These cases involved the Louisville airport expansion and, earlier, the construction of the all-important Toyota Plant in Georgetown. This large facility has now been expanded three times, employs more than six thousand people and has attracted scores of parts suppliers to service Kentucky's growing auto manufacturing base. Both projects were game changers for the state's economy.

In the Toyota decision, known as *Hayes v. State Property and Buildings Commission*, Stephens framed a ruling approving the constitutionality of state incentives that resulted in the creation of thousands of new jobs in the state. This decision penned by Stephens grew out of Governor Martha Layne Collins's steps to encourage Toyota to build in Scott County near Georgetown, Kentucky, where a sprawling auto manufacturing plant was ultimately located. There were concerns at the time as to the constitutionality of spending state funds to benefit a private company, but in a stroke of brilliance, the Collins administration used the strategy of having the state's finance secretary, Larry Hayes, sue the governor in a case that made the expected incentives the central issue.

The Kentucky Supreme Court ruled 4-3 in an opinion by Chief Justice Stephens that the use of state funds for the project fortunately was constitutional. Yet another example of Stephens stretching the constitution with the ingenious argument that the state, contrary to the argument that it was unconstitutionally providing funds to a private corporation, was going to get the benefit of the bargain from incremental state and local property taxes and increased income taxes from new employment. When asked her opinion of the decision by the press shortly after it came down, Governor Collins simply stated, "I'm just glad it's over."[96]

As a result of this opinion, a succession of eight governors with bipartisan votes of overwhelming majorities of both legislative houses have enacted and expanded versions of these tax credit programs, beginning in 1989 with the passage of a bill creating the Kentucky Rural Economic Development Authority (KREDA), which Governors Patton and Wilkinson championed. Political leaders in both parties embraced tax credits to encourage businesses to locate in Kentucky and expand under similar programs for the service and technology sectors, urban areas and existing industries. Even now, Kentucky is likely in negotiations with companies wanting to use these incentives that are undeniably useful but which are monitored by the press and the attorney general to ensure that the state gets the benefits for its bargain.

These incentives later came under withering attack by the federal judiciary in 2004 in a case known as *Daimler Chrysler v. Cuno*. Then Kentucky attorney Greg Stumbo (D-Prestonsburg) made a critical move to join other states in appealing to the 6th Circuit Court of Appeals a decision declaring unconstitutional an Ohio statute granting tax credits used to promote economic development as violating the commerce clause of the U.S. Constitution. Stumbo was concerned that the Court's ruling might deter businesses considering a move to Kentucky and jeopardize his state's job development and competitiveness with surrounding states relying on tax incentives in the competition for economic growth.

Stumbo, and one of his deputy attorney generals, Pierce Whites, made the case that Kentucky would be at a disadvantage if the Court ruled against these incentives and could be forced to consider a return to the inefficient means of attracting jobs with direct cash outlays from the state treasury. This case later wound its way to the U.S. Supreme Court, which unanimously ruled that state taxpayers, in this case Mr. Cuno, did not have standing under Article III of the federal Constitution to challenge state tax or spending decisions related to economic development. Kentucky and other states thus dodged a bullet in this decision and avoided the need to return to cash outlays as incentives or issuing more debt with state bonds.

An adverse decision in this case would have been disastrous given the state's fiscal crisis in 2004 and because Kentucky simply could not compete effectively with surrounding states with larger tax bases. Time and again, Kentucky saw that while factors such as an educated workforce and an integrated transportation system are key considerations in site selection for business, the availability of meaningful tax credits on an otherwise level playing field can tip the balance in negotiations for job growth. The tax credit advantage helped Kentucky land large deals. These included United Parcel Service's hub in Louisville, General Motors in Bowling Green with a Corvette plant, Mountain Top Baking Company in Pike County (later owned by Kellogg's) and hundreds of other companies persuaded to locate businesses in Kentucky and create more jobs thanks to these incentives.

As Paul Patton first argued as lieutenant governor and as economic development secretary, and it became evident as these programs evolved, the success of tax incentives lies in their structure and the monitoring of their implementation to ensure compliance with investment and job requirements. Rather than the old way of providing companies with cash outlays with no certainty that a company would create the jobs it promised, Kentucky tax credits provide benefits only when businesses make their promised capital investments and generate earnings.

Just as important, however, is the fact that the tax credits are provided against taxes the state would otherwise have realized had these jobs not been created in Kentucky in the first place. Businesses that do not achieve their employment commitments face stiff penalties, but if they make their promised investment, Kentucky realizes the added benefit of secondary jobs and new payroll, sales, property and other taxes.

Robert F. Stephens, chief justice of the Kentucky Supreme Court, 1979–99. *Public domain.*

The number of jobs and investment created for Kentucky-based workers, thanks largely to the creativity of Chief Justice Stephens in the 1985 Toyota opinion upholding state incentives for private development, is long and legendary. The message was and remains clear: the creation of jobs through Kentucky's tax incentive programs positively affects our economy and serves to enhance our commerce among the states and the nation.

All of this is to say, time and again, that Kentucky's judiciary—at the district and circuit court levels, at the Court of Appeals, in the Kentucky Supreme Court and the state's two federal court districts—repeatedly played a leading role paving the way for Kentucky's landmark reforms. And often at the center of these reforms were the decisions of Chief Justice Robert Stephens interpreting Kentucky's separation of powers provisions. The legality of such steps toward progress was inspired by Jefferson's articulation of separation of powers, as integrated into the state constitution.

Chapter 11

KENTUCKY'S CONSTITUTION
AND THE BUDGET HELD HOSTAGE

Does Jefferson's Legacy Hold Lessons When Congress Deadlocks on the Budget?

Anyone following the news even casually cannot help but notice that Congress increasingly finds itself unable to agree on a budget, at times flat-lining expenditures for months with a procedural device known as a "continuing resolution." Often this time is used for wrangling on various political affairs, resulting as it did with the ouster of the House Speaker Kevin McCarthy in 2023. Stalemates occur as the parties fight over twelve separate appropriations measures instead of agreeing on an annual fiscal year budget to begin October 1. When Congress yet again reached this fiscal cliff in 2023, we heard from the White House a new idea: for the executive branch to issue a spending plan in the event of a Congressional impasse.

In 2002, Kentucky found itself in nearly the same place when Governor Paul Patton issued a spending plan by executive order when Kentucky's General Assembly, dominated in the Senate by Republicans and in the House under Democrats, failed to adopt a budget prior to Kentucky's fiscal year starting July 1. At that time, an op-ed was published in the *Louisville Courier-Journal* ruminating on the question of whether the governor could issue a spending plan by executive order, suggesting that the state's constitution, and specifically Jefferson's legacy in that document under Sections 27 and 28, offered helpful guidance.[97]

Indeed, in the spring of 2002, as the General Assembly neared its end, Kentucky for the first time did not have a legislatively enacted budget. Certain operations of government needed to go forward, and Governor Patton believed that emergency expenditures may be essential despite the fact that other states and the courts provided little guidance in developing a spending plan. At the time, Kentucky conducted a political exercise the Biden White House and the Democrats must have considered recently when the nation was looking at another fiscal cliff through an inability of Congress to increase the debt limit on expenditures. To remedy the impasse in Kentucky, Governor Patton looked carefully at the state constitution, its separations of powers provisions and case law, interpreting them to develop an emergency spending plan.

Gradually, with the advice of the state's foremost constitutional scholars, Patton became convinced that the state constitution provided him ground on which to issue a spending plan by executive order that would maintain the operations of state government. Kentucky's constitution, like the nation's, has clauses (in Kentucky under Sections 69 and 81) vesting supreme executive power in the governor "to take care that the laws be faithfully executed." Patton argued, as would Biden, that revenues for public purposes were vital to see that laws were carried out and properly funded, the sworn duty of the chief magistrate of the commonwealth. While this interpretation seemed to run afoul of Jefferson's view of separation of powers, could the authority of the executive branch be stretched in an emergency?

Under these clauses, coupled with state constitutional provisions requiring a balanced budget, Patton felt that he could carry on operations if the General Assembly failed to pass a budget to do so. That Kentucky's constitution is unusually detailed as compared to the federal charter or those of other states is indeed fortunate. Jefferson's contributions to the work of the framers is not insignificant. While our courts through the years emphasized that Sections 27 and 28 in our state constitution prohibit one branch of government from interfering with responsibilities of another, what if one branch were unwilling to execute its constitutional duty to appropriate funds?

This question was raised in a case considered by the Kentucky Court of Appeals eighty years ago, and its outcome may be instructional for Congress today. In this case, known as *Miller v. Quertermous* (1947), the General Assembly was challenged for not adequately appropriating critical funding for the operation of state hospitals. In its decision, the Court held that this function of state government must continue and that if the General Assembly failed to appropriate necessary funds, it would "say that the state's moral sense of responsibility is either non-existent or atrophied."[98]

The Court went on to approve expenses for the operation of government under an existing budget and in circumstances far less critical than the current impasse in Congress or in Kentucky in 2002, when there was no budget at all. In the Court's opinion, it was specifically noted that while Section 230 of Kentucky's constitution provides that "no money shall be withdrawn from the state treasury except in pursuance of appropriations made by law," this clause should "not be so narrowly limited as to mean that the legislature has exclusive control."[99]

Our courts therefore have provided needed flexibility to this document to address the obvious imperative that critical services of government must continue when Kentucky, or in current times the nation, experiences a budget impasse. At this time, this author, then the governor's general counsel, summarized a view on the governor's authority to implement a spending plan within an executive order, as follows:

MEMORANDUM

To: Governor Paul Patton

FROM: Denis Fleming

DATE: April 3, 2002

RE: Governor's Emergency Powers in a Budget Impasse

SUMMARY

I have reviewed state and federal law relative to the question of what emergency powers the Governor of Kentucky has to expend funds in the public interest should the General Assembly fail to enact a budget by July 1, 2002. This question requires a review of the Governor's power that is dependent upon the Constitution and the General Assembly and secondly to what extent does the Governor have implied or inherent powers in addition to those expressly given him by law. For the following reasons I have concluded that following an exhaustion of legislative options, the Governor may, temporarily, and upon a carefully defined basis, exercise emergency powers under KRS Chapter 39 and Kentucky Supreme Court precedent to expend public funds in the interest of public safety and for the preservation of necessary governmental functions until such time as the General Assembly can exercise its constitutional duty to enact a budget. (See Miller v. Quertermous 202 SW3d 289 (1947). (Here the Ky. Court of Appeals noted that while Sec. 230 of the Constitution provides no money shall be drawn from the state treasury except in pursuance of appropriations made by law, this should not be "so narrowly limited as to mean that the Legislature has exclusive control." The Court further held that if "there was a Legislative refusal to appropriate" there may be a "moral sense of responsibility" for the Courts or the Executive to make payments for necessary government expenditures.) (Copy of decision attached) Absent this limited circumstance, there is little legal authority for a more expansive interpretation of executive authority even in an emergency outside of what is granted to him by law.[100]

Patton thus proceeded with a spending plan by executive order consistent with the key features of the legislature's budget bill. One may ask the obvious question: What is the check on the governor's authority to adopt the spending plan in the absence of legislative approval? Again, we can look to the state constitution, which provides under Section 2 that arbitrary and capricious power over the lives of our citizens shall not be exercised by government and that our court system is the check on the exercise of this power through its lawful responsibility to interpret the state constitution and likewise for the federal courts to interpret the federal Constitution.

Unfortunately, budget negotiations in 2002 broke down in a dispute over election finance reform. Often budget negotiations break down over a particular issue, as happened in Congress 2023 over funding for Ukraine or as could happen at any time over a particular aspect of the budget. Election finance reform was enacted in Kentucky by the General Assembly in 1992 and was hailed as a progressive step in response to a rather sordid if not colorful history of vote buying.

This 1992 law was part of an effort that included a rare amendment to Kentucky's constitution in Section 70, which requires slating of candidates for governor and lieutenant governor, a key feature of the campaign finance law. Several states still have some form of full or partial funding for elections, although the trend has been away from these laws in recent years on First Amendment grounds.

Kentucky's law at the time was designed to limit expenditures, with caps on spending and contributions, and contained a trigger provision that provided a two-to-one dollar match to participating gubernatorial slates should a wealthy candidate opt out of the program and spend over the limitations. Several outside groups, including the Republican Party, tested key provisions of this law in federal court, and it was repeatedly upheld by federal district and appeals courts. The philosophy of the law proved successful and without question limited expenditures in gubernatorial elections and engaged the public in a discussion of the issues.

There was a flurry of activity in 2002 litigating this budget issue in Franklin Circuit Court, which Louisville lawyer Sheryl Snyder helped with immeasurably in his representation of Governor Patton. As the litigation progressed, Kentucky went nearly a year without an enacted budget. In a last-ditch effort to save public financing for gubernatorial slates, the parties came to an agreement, a budget was enacted in 2003 and public financing in gubernatorial races in Kentucky went by the wayside. Prior to this agreement however, much preparation had been made to implement a budget for the state by executive order in the event a compromise failed.

The leadership of the departments of government submitted their budgets to the state budget office, and the governor carefully reviewed the proposed budget and made reasonable changes; the document was circulated and prepared for issuance. Arguably, the state was at a point of constitutional crisis in which one branch of government, the legislature, failed for political reasons to do its duty. This occurred as another branch under our tripod system, the executive, proposed to go forward by fulfilling an essentially legislative duty in an emergency. Then the whole matter was presented to the third branch, the judiciary, for a decision as to whether it was constitutional. Kentucky in 2002 went much farther down the road toward a constitutional crisis than the nation entertained in 2023.

But the story did not end there. In 2004, under Kentucky governor Ernie Fletcher, the General Assembly yet again found itself in a party deadlock and adjourned without enacting a budget bill. The governor in this instance did not call a special session of the legislature to address the issue but did proceed as Governor Patton before him and issued a budget by executive order called the Public Services Continuation Plan. Franklin Circuit Court within a few months declared the plan unconstitutional, and the matter found itself before the Supreme Court in 2005. In this instance, the Court relied on Sections 27 and 28 of Kentucky's constitution, the separation of powers provisions, and—quoting previous opinions—referred to them as an unusually forceful command. Jefferson's authorship of these provisions of the constitution again were mentioned by the Supreme Court directly in the opinion.

In some interesting language, the Supreme Court stated, "When the General Assembly declines to exercise its appropriations power, that power does not flow over the high wall" erected by Section 28 to another department of government. In other words, Section 28 could not be stretched to empower a governor to encroach on the constitutionally mandated power of another branch, that being the legislature, which is the sole entity empowered to make appropriations. Jefferson may have been proud given his original concerns 220 years ago with the dangers of an overpowerful executive born of his distrust of King George as reflected in the Declaration of Independence.[101]

In the right circumstance, Kentucky could prove itself a reasonable precedent for legal and political reasons for a strong executive, if necessary, to proceed with necessary expenditures to operate the national government. In fact, the nation flirted with the very constitutional crisis Jefferson sought to avoid with his separation of powers provisions more than once in the twenty-first century. In 2020, for example, Congress was in gridlock over a second stimulus bill to provide relief during the coronavirus epidemic.

At that time, President Trump issued four executive orders in August of that year directing the spending of federal dollars for unemployment benefits and a payroll tax cut when Congress stalled in its negotiations on a stimulus during the pandemic. The orders were extensive and included additional protections for renters that might be evicted from their homes, suspension of student loan payments and related appropriations. These actions were immediately attacked as to whether Trump had the constitutional authority to issue the orders or even the money to pay for them absent a Congressional appropriation, which the federal Constitution mandates.

Lawrence Tribe, Professor Emeritus at Harvard Law School and nationally recognized constitutional scholar, called Trump's executive orders not only "cynical" but also unconstitutional and stated publicly, "He obviously has no legal power to do that. But daring anyone to take him to court might be good politics."[102] In 2002, the nearly identical budget matter was taken to state court in Kentucky and arguably resulted in good politics. The bold decision of Governor Patton to go forward not only with certain expenditures not approved by the legislature but also the entirety of the state budget precipitated a retreat by the General Assembly and eventual enactment of a state budget.

One can only speculate on how a federal court might address this matter had President Biden, President Trump or another president decided to go forward with the nation's budget issued by executive order when Congress reaches an impasse. As a general matter, Congress has the power to overturn an executive order by passing legislation that invalidates it, just as it can reject executive administrative regulations that exceed congressionally delegated authority. Courts can likewise strike down executive orders or regulations on constitutional grounds, and Congress can always refuse to provide, under the Constitution's appropriations clause, Article I, Section 9, the funding to carry out policies contained in an executive order. But in considering the prospect of a constitutional budget crisis, and the absence in our federal Constitution of separation of powers clauses as Jefferson favored in Kentucky and Virginia's constitutions, federal courts may stretch to reach a legally supported outcome.

It's likewise speculative but possible to make a guess as to what Jefferson may have concluded regarding modern-day budget practices. As we have seen, he was concerned with a large concentration of power in any one branch of government based on his study of the British constitution and his experience in France as the nation's minister to that country, when the monarchy had great power. All this may have fueled his efforts to explicitly protect the integrity of each branch of government by proposing separation of powers clauses in constitutional documents.

While Jefferson himself struggled with periods of personal debt, when it came to governmental spending, he was greatly concerned with deficit practices. In a long letter to President George Washington in September 1792, Jefferson as secretary of state lamented the national debt, stating, "I would wish the debt be paid tomorrow," and that "no man is more ardently intent to see the public debt paid soon and sacredly paid off than I am."[103]

He fretted over the cost of the Louisiana Purchase, which temporarily put the nation in debt, but he viewed that acquisition as a pivotal moment of national security as he envisioned the westward expansion of a great nation. Jefferson notably later flirted with a constitutional amendment prohibiting the federal government from incurring any debt much like the balanced budget provisions that have long been in Kentucky's constitution.

He had studied not just the flaws he saw in the British constitution concentrating fiscal power heavily in the monarchy. He also believed that the expansion of government debt would lead the country into "an English career of debt, corruption, and rottenness, closing with revolution." It's very possible that Jefferson may have viewed the idea of simply printing new money to meet the government's obligations as a substitute to cutting expenditures or even raising taxes as an unacceptable practice, economically if not constitutionally infirm.[104]

CRIMINAL JUSTICE REFORM ADOPTING JEFFERSON'S PRINCIPLES, THE PARDON POWER AND STATE EXECUTIONS

In addition to his fascination with the dynamics among the branches of government and how to protect the integrity of these branches in state constitutions, Jefferson had a keen interest in the criminal justice system and the extent to which state constitutions should address them. In 1778, Jefferson proposed to the Virginia legislature "A Bill for Proportioning Crimes and Punishments." Jefferson initiated this project of criminal justice reform shortly after his writing of the Declaration of Independence when he had returned to Virginia. Several features of this detailed initiative were later brought to Kentucky and used by John Breckinridge in his own reform of the criminal justice system. This reform was enacted by the General Assembly in the 1790s, not long after Kentucky was admitted to the Union.

Jefferson believed in second chances, rehabilitation of criminals to return to society and the limited if not reluctant use of capital punishment. Jefferson did not oppose the death penalty, but he set about limiting it in Virginia, which at the time he considered these laws itemized thirty-nine crimes subject to the death penalty, including the stealing of a cabbage. Jefferson's progressive view on criminal justice matters is well summarized in a portion of his proposed reform of the Virginia Penal Code (1778) in the preamble to "A Bill for Proportioning Crimes and Punishments":

> *And whereas the Reformation of offenders although an object worthy of the attention of the laws, is not affected at all by capital punishments, which exterminate instead of reforming, and should be the last melancholy*

*resource against those whose existence is become inconsistent with the safety
of their fellow citizens, which also weakened the state by cutting off so
many who, if reformed, might be restored sound members to society, who,
even under a course of correction, might be rendered useful in various labors
for the public, and would be living and long continued spectacles to deter
others from committing the like offenses.*[105]

This statement is essentially a summary of his considered views on the
potential for reformation of criminal offenders. Jefferson was a man well read
on a variety of matters and is understood to have considered the thinking of
the legendary Italian jurist and philosopher Cesare Beccaria (1738–1794).
Beccaria was ahead of his time, arguing the immorality of the death penalty
and even cruel and unusual punishments. His principal notion of the role
of the state in criminal justice was to punish truly dangerous offenders but
also to rehabilitate eligible offenders, maintain social order and give people
a second chance.

Beccaria's influence on Jefferson can be seen in those aspects of his
proposed penal reform for Virginia that he incorporated into that state's
first constitution. Beccaria's landmark 1764 treatise, titled *On Crimes and
Punishments*, was translated into English and may have been studied by
Jefferson in the original Italian, which is one of several languages that
interested him.

One of the precepts Beccaria set forth in his treatise was the seemingly
obvious notion that punishments for crimes should be fixed in law, as
opposed to being applied arbitrarily. It's conjecture but possible that the
extraordinary length and specificity of Jefferson's proposed penal code and
Virginia's constitutional section on crimes and punishment are outgrowths
of his study of Beccaria's precepts. While it does not appear that John
Breckinridge carried over this specificity in criminal justice laws to the
Kentucky Constitution, it's likely that he brought to Kentucky the principles
of reform he saw Jefferson propose for Virginia criminal law and used them
in his own state in the 1790s.

It is evident that Jefferson struggled with the proper balance in the
imposition of penalties for criminal behavior and struggled particularly with
the death penalty. His belief, perhaps derived from readings of Beccaria
and other eighteenth-century jurists, was that people give up their "social
contract," in other words their rights to freedom and life, only under the
condition of aggravated murder and treason against the country. His penal
code and proposed construct for Virginia's constitution set forth what today

seems to be an unusual enumeration of crimes subject to punishment and the death penalty, with treason being a focus. This may be understandable, as these documents were prepared when the United States was in the midst of its Revolutionary War with Great Britain. Jefferson and Breckinridge, both of whom championed a balanced criminal justice reform in their states, would have been fascinated to know that two hundred years later, Kentucky applied these principles to a landmark reform of its criminal justice system in 1998.

A major reform two years in the making and hailed as a success at the time was the enactment by the Kentucky General Assembly in 1998 of House Bill 455 (criminal justice reform legislation). At the time, this bill, which became known as the Kentucky Criminal Justice Reform Act, was and remains the most sweeping reform of criminal justice in fifty years. The bill brought balance to the justice and prison systems with reforms of adult and juvenile sentencing; life without parole was established for serious offenses, and diversion programs were established for nonviolent offenders. This was a comprehensive example of the modern-day application of the progressive reforms in criminal justice envisioned and written into law by Jefferson and Breckinridge two hundred years earlier.[106]

The effort to provide balance to a criminal justice system and to not under- or overreact was constant. For example, in the wake of several church burnings at the time in Kentucky, the state attorney general, Ben Chandler, established a task force with Patton that recommended enhanced penalties for hate crimes of this nature. Gang violence prevailed in the summers of 1997 and 1998 in Lexington and more so in Louisville. Louisville mayor Jerry Abramson, who was highly regarded, called Governor Patton in the summer of 1997 and indicated concern with gang violence and murders in the city, which at that point exceeded seventy for the year. He had an idea that Patton supported to temporarily deploy Kentucky state troopers to patrol the interstate system in Louisville to free up additional city officers to patrol the city's highly violent areas. This proved not only to be helpful to the city but also sparked an initiative in the Governor's Office and among members of the General Assembly to deal legislatively with gang violence as part of a larger crime package.

While the Criminal Justice Reform Bill in 1997 was being formulated for introduction in 1998, Patton and Chandler worked to add provisions to the crime bill that would have criminalized patterns of gang activity where the intent to conspire to commit violent or financial crimes could be proven with a certain number of participants. Strong arguments were made by members of the General Assembly and the minority community against this bill as being unduly targeted from an equal protection and due process standpoint.

Although it was modified, the gang violence provisions of the much larger criminal justice reform bill were not included in the legislation. It is notable that the Kentucky General Assembly in 2018 enacted its own version of a state Racketeer Influenced Corrupt Organizations Act (RICO) applicable to patterns of gang and other criminal enterprises. A version of this RICO legislation was used in Georgia to prosecute former president Trump and his associates.

Later, when he was in Congress, Ben Chandler followed up on his work in criminal justice reform by introducing a bill modeled on the similar mechanism of enhanced penalties for crimes, this time protecting the nation's seniors from abuse. The Elder Abuse Protection Act of 2009 (HR1374) served to strengthen penalties for those convicted of violent offenses against seniors. The mechanism became a model for other state and federal criminal justice laws.

The preparation of the Kentucky criminal justice reform law was an ordeal. It was a nearly two-year process that brought to life the struggles Jefferson had as to what the proper balance should be for crimes and punishments in state law and under a state constitution. These struggles involved the extent to which minor offenses should be overlooked, the diversion of offenders to programs of rehabilitation, the extent of punishment, the length of incarceration for serious crimes and a consideration of the death penalty.

In 1997 through 1998, the process of preparing this bill on justice reform involved every major organization of prosecutors, defense attorneys and judges one could imagine. Fayette County attorney Ray Larson in Lexington and Chief Justice Stephens were consulted; the state Prosecutors Advisory Council, Dean Robert Lawson of the University of Kentucky College of Law (the preeminent criminal law and procedure professor) and others were brought in. Also, earlier in the Patton administration, he had reformed the juvenile justice system at the insistence of the Department of Justice and Attorney General Janet Reno, who visited the state twice to encourage it. As a result, HB455 included additional revisions to the juvenile justice system to give juveniles a second chance in appropriate circumstances. The structure of the criminal justice system in Kentucky began to gradually shift toward the principles of balance and rehabilitation of offenders, which Jefferson and Breckinridge proposed more than two hundred years earlier.

Moreover, these notions were a matter of personal interest of the governor, who believed strongly in some instances that juveniles should be given a second chance in life. Patton opposed the juvenile death penalty, despite the 1989 decision of the U.S. Supreme Court in *Stanford v. Kentucky*. This case upheld imposition of the death penalty on offenders who were at least sixteen at the time of the crime. Some of Patton's interest in fair juvenile laws was a result of his own run-in with the law as a youth when he was arrested for stealing tires. He long believed in a second chance for everybody, which was an endearing quality about him. HB455 ultimately passed the General Assembly, and a widely attended signing ceremony was held in the Rotunda of the state capitol in the summer of 1998.

Among Patton's more somber criminal justice work was dealing with death penalty cases and death row inmates. Kentucky, like many states, has a convoluted death penalty appeals process that allows the defendant continually to appeal portions of a lower court decision, pushing execution dates decades into the future. Part of the effort to accelerate this process was the aggressive work of Attorney General Chandler in sending letters to Patton asking him to set the execution date of inmates that in his legal judgment should have been carried forth.

Two death row inmates were executed at Eddyville State Penitentiary during the Patton administration: Harold McQueen Jr. in 1997 and Eddie Lee Harper in 1999. McQueen was convicted of murdering a convenience store clerk, twenty-two-year-old Rebecca O'Hearn in Richmond, Kentucky, in 1980, shooting her twice point blank in the face and in the back of the head.

Other circumstances of the crime made it egregious, but because of the lengthy appellate process, McQueen was not considered for execution until 1997. The governor approached this case in a methodical way, frequently asking to review the files before ultimately signing a death warrant for McQueen's execution. This took place on July 1, 1997, in the electric chair at Eddyville. The McQueen execution was a matter of controversy, with many people and interest groups visiting or wanting to visit with the governor on either side of the issue. It divided some members of the Governor's Office staff, who for reasons related to the death penalty opted to not participate in the case discussions.

McQueen's death warrant became more challenging when the governor received a nineteen-minute videotape message from McQueen in which he discussed his religious conversion, his new spiritual path, his work in prison and battle with drugs, some of which he was on at the time of the murder. This brought forth the very struggles Jefferson had in limiting the use of the death penalty in Virginia, and his interest and the potential for the rehabilitation of criminals that Breckinridge in the late 1790s helped enact in Kentucky's criminal law. McQueen was the first execution carried out in Kentucky since 1962.

Because of the difficulties with the electrocution of McQueen, Eddie Lee Harper was executed in 1999 by lethal injection, which had its own complications. Harper was a thirty-three-year-old, twice-divorced, laid-off machinist who was financially insecure and convicted in Jefferson County of shooting his adoptive parents to death with a .38-caliber handgun on February 19, 1982. It was an egregious crime, and prosecutors proved an elaborate plan of premeditation centered on trying to make the crime look like a burglary gone bad so Harper could inherit his parents' estate, valued at $85,000. While the law was carried out in both these instances of execution, they were somber matters. Not to mention that this penalty was carried out years after the crimes were committed.

Later, in the 2002 session of the General Assembly, Patton supported a groundbreaking bill to eliminate the death penalty for juveniles. While this legislation failed, Patton on his final day in office commuted the death sentence of Kevin Stanford, whom the Supreme Court had ruled could be executed for the 1981 brutal rape, sodomy and murder of a gas station attendant in Louisville. Stanford was seventeen at the time, and the case concerned a particularly heinous murder. Much later, in 2005, the U.S. Supreme Court overruled *Stanford v. Kentucky*, which had sanctioned the juvenile death penalty. Stanford's death sentence was commuted to life in prison without parole. At the time, he had been on death row for twenty years.

This decision by the U.S. Supreme Court in *Roper v. Simmons*, which referenced the commutation by Patton of Stanford's sentence, held that the Eighth and Fourteenth Amendments to the federal Constitution forbid imposition of the death penalty on offenders under age eighteen when their crimes were committed. Despite the egregious crime of Stanford, the prescient thinking of the governor was rooted in his compassion for juveniles who committed crimes, his own experience and his belief that people are entitled to a second chance. Although centuries apart, this was similar to the sentiments on this issue of Jefferson, Breckinridge and Beccaria about punishment levels and the potential for rehabilitation of those convicted of heinous offenses.[107]

A final matter somewhat lost in history was Patton's determined effort in 2002 to pardon en masse hundreds of jailed criminals for what arguably were moderate offenses. This took place at a time when he tried but failed to have previously passed systemic tax reform. The state had entered a period of mild recession, and the legislature at this time was split, with the Senate being controlled by Republicans and the House still in Democratic control.

The governor made a mighty effort and indeed passed in the House major tax reform, which would have brought more than $400 million per year into the state coffers, which was a good deal of money in 2002 dollars. This was the backdrop for a budget crunch as part of the governor's calculation in considering a prison release for some criminals was financial. However, he tried to identify criminals who were eligible for early release and might have a good path toward rehabilitation. This was a hotly debated issue internally, with profound implications in Kentucky if not nationally as to the proper use of the pardon power—or, in this matter, the power to commute a criminal sentence.

The source of the power of the governor to commute a criminal sentence is found in Section 77 of Kentucky's constitution. It is straightforward but has resulted in a surprising degree of litigation, which continues to surface the more governors exercise the power. Section 77 ("Power of Governor to remit fines and forfeitures, grant reprieves and pardons—no power to remit fees") states:

> *He shall have power to remit fines and forfeitures, commute sentences, grant reprieves and pardons, except in case of impeachment, and he shall file with each application therefore a statement of the reasons for his decision thereon, which application and statement shall always be open to public inspection.*

The executive order commuting the sentences of 567 Kentucky state prison inmates was prepared referencing this section of the constitution and related sections in support of the executive powers of a governor. On the morning of December 19, 2002, the order was filed, and the first of 567 prison inmates began to be released from state jails, largely in a step to reduce a $500 million budget deficit. Some in the administration opposed this executive order, which was prepared with the governor and experts in the justice cabinet. Patton stressed in his press release that only nonviolent offenders were being given early release by commutation, but several of them appeared to be career criminals. When he announced the commutations, Patton expressed his concern about recidivism and stated, "A percentage of them are going to recommit a crime and some of them are going to be worse than the crimes they are in for. I have to do what I have to do to live within the revenue that we have."[108]

While the order was carried out by prison officials, it was quickly rescinded when some paroled criminals committed crimes upon their release, including an attempted bank robbery. Fortunately, the order was structured as a phased release of inmates should unacceptable numbers of released inmates begin to commit crimes. This difficult experience played a role at the end of the administration in 2003 when Governor Patton spent large portions of weeks before the inauguration of Governor Fletcher in considering but rejecting more than one hundred people for gubernatorial pardons or sentence commutations.

Patton worked constantly, refining a list of those he would consider for a pardon or commutation, and there were stacks of case files he was regularly reviewing. In the end, a day or two before the end of the administration, his staff found him one morning shaking his head and saying that he just did not think he would do any of them. Word had gotten out that he was considering pardons, and the governor and his staff were besieged by defense attorneys and family members of convicted criminals seeking relief.

Later, at the end of Governor Matt Bevin's administration, this governor issued a series of highly controversial pardons in some cases of individuals who returned to society only to recommit offenses. It was this perceived abuse, documented in a Pulitzer Prize–winning series by the *Louisville Courier-Journal*, that motivated the General Assembly in 2024 to propose legislation placing limitations on the pardon power of the governor. Because this power is derived from explicit provisions in Kentucky's constitution, this legislation, not yet passed at this writing, would put to the voters the question as to whether they favor a change in the state constitution relating to pardons and the commutation of sentences. Here is yet another example of the constant tensions among the branches of government when one perceives the other has exceeded its authority.

DINNER WITH EIGHT KENTUCKY GOVERNORS ON CONSTITUTIONAL REFORM AT THE GOVERNOR'S MANSION

As a result of an amendment to Kentucky's constitution, in 1992, Paul Patton was the first sitting governor to serve two consecutive four year terms except for the anomaly of Governor James Garrard (1796–1804).[109] Succession for Kentucky's governors was an item debated by John Breckinridge and others at the 1799 constitutional convention, and despite eventually being in our federal Constitution, the idea was nevertheless discarded in favor a of a single four-year term.

Jefferson went back and forth on what he thought best for the tenure of the governor of Virginia in his proposed constitution for that state in 1778, and the founding fathers debated how the tenure of the president should be handled in the federal Constitution. Some states such as Massachusetts first proposed the tenure of their governor be as short as one year. Other states settled on one term of four years, as did Kentucky, but most reflected what became the Twenty-Second Amendment to the federal Constitution on the presidency by limiting the terms of a governor at two consecutive four-year terms. Still others, such as Louisiana, have no constitutional limit on a governor's term at all.

While Patton did not take reelection for granted and intended to campaign as hard as necessary to win, in the spring of 1999, prior to his reelection, he felt it prudent to prepare for the 2000 session of the General Assembly. Assuming he won a second term, with an experienced administration in place, a good relationship with the legislature and four more years to implement a program, he sensed an opportunity to make big policy changes in Kentucky. Sitting in the Governor's Office in January 1999, he spoke about some of his ideas to the secretary of his cabinet, Crit Luallen; his chief of staff, Andrew "Skipper" Martin; his general counsel (this writer); and Jack Conway, the cabinet's top lawyer.

First among these was to host a series of discussions with serious thinkers on opportunities available to Kentucky as it began a new century. Because so much had been written on whether Kentucky's constitution needed further reform, he decided to devote an evening of discussion to this topic with distinguished scholars and jurists. Governor Patton and Luallen knew most of these scholars and jurists well and began to list them.

Prior to this, however, he landed on a bolder idea, which was to assemble all seven of the living former governors of Kentucky for dinner at the Governor's Mansion to discuss state constitutional reform and other policy initiatives. Some of the initiatives he wished to cover were systemic tax reform, further improvement in education building on his post-secondary education reform, amending the state constitution to authorize the General Assembly to permit municipal home rule for counties, casino gambling and annual sessions of the General Assembly.

He did not view this as an exercise in posturing, and as far as he was concerned, it was to be off the record at the time. He wanted to benefit from the candid views of each of the governors as he began to formulate an agenda for the next four years. In preparation for this meeting, he mailed everyone a copy of *A Citizens Guide to the Kentucky Constitution*, published by the Legislative Research Commission (LRC) in 1993. Sheryl Snyder, leading constitutional law expert, was consulted in advance of the dinner for his thoughts and direction on this meeting. The governor asked his staff to organize the dinner through his administrative assistant, Sally Flynn; prepare a letter of invitation and a draft agenda; and to work with Luallen and Martin. To everyone's amazement, every living governor except Wallace G. Wilkinson (1988–91) attended the dinner.

The day approached for the great dinner, and the governor wondered about whether this might be the largest gathering of governors of any one state in the nation's history. It very well may have been. In addition to his general counsel, Luallen, Martin and Lieutenant Governor Steve Henry, the governors in attendance, as seen from the photo on the next page, were Edward T. "Ned" Breathitt, 1963–67; Louie Nunn, 1967–71; Wendell Ford, 1971–75; Julian Carroll, 1975–80; John Y. Brown Jr., 1980–84; Martha Layne Collins, 1984–88; Brereton Jones, 1991–95; and Paul Patton, 1995–2003.

The afternoon of the dinner, Governor Patton called his general counsel into his office and asked him to take careful notes of the meeting. The

Eight governors of Kentucky, First Lady Judi Patton, Cabinet Secretary Crit Luallen, Chief of Staff Skipper Martin and Counsel Denis Fleming at the Governor's Mansion, 1999. *Photo in possession of the author.*

evening began with the invitees in the Parlor Room off the main entrance to the Governor's Mansion starting at 6:00 p.m. For ninety minutes, there was a rollicking discussion among all the governors about a variety of matters that Governor Patton tried to moderate, although at times he had to mitigate the strong opinions. A copy of one page of the notes taken during this discussion is set forth in the illustrations. A good deal of discussion initially centered on the idea of legislating merged government, in other words city county mergers with a permissive amendment to the Kentucky Constitution. This would allow communities greater economies of scale in public services, theoretically lower taxes and create efficiencies in budgeting.

Every governor was in favor of this reform, with Governor Breathitt arguing strongly that Kentucky needed to amend its state constitution and with Governor Nunn saying that it needed to be left to the communities, although both John Y. Brown and Brereton Jones felt strongly that Louisville could be the catalyst for reform. At that time, both leaders in Louisville, Mayor Jerry Abramson and County Judge-Executive David Armstrong, supported merged government, while many felt that a 1994 constitutional amendment allowed such mergers to proceed upon approval

Governor's Dinner

February 1999

Breathitt:
⇒ Debated Combs on succession - he argued for it.
⇒ Merged governments - would be a big plus - need to amend Constitution to allow for this.

L. Nunn:
⇒ Leave it to local community.

JY Brown:
⇒ Louisville catalyst - get merger done

B. Jones:
⇒ Both leaders in Louisville support

Ford:
⇒ Get Congressional support - and - General Assembly support.
⇒ "Good idea"; its how you get it done.

Patton:
⇒ Can get rural legislators to get it done.

Annual Sessions

J Carroll:
⇒ A full time legislator when you get a _____ - Legislature will run things.

Breathitt:
⇒ Named leadership in 1963 -

J Carroll:
⇒ LRC v. Brown is _____ .

Casino Gambling

B Jones:
⇒ Vote as constitutional amendment
⇒ Allow it at horse tracks only, not video terminals.

JY Brown:
⇒ Favors ult's
⇒ lecture on computer gambling - internets doing it.

Partial transcript of notes by the author from the meeting of eight Kentucky governors in 1999 on constitutional reform. *In possession of the author.*

of the General Assembly. City-county merged government ultimately was approved by the General Assembly and the voters in Louisville in 2000. Other communities in Kentucky followed or had already done so, such as Lexington, and it allowed Kentucky cities to compete economically with cities in the region that had long since realized this reform such as Indianapolis and Nashville.

The dinner with former governors that February 1999 went on to be quite lively on the discussion of annual sessions of the General Assembly. Former governor Carroll opposed this, having been a strong governor himself, because he felt that a full-time legislature "will just run everything." Years later, the notion of annual sessions became a hot topic in discussions in the basement of the Governor's Mansion with House and Senate leadership and even Supreme Court chief justice Stephens. Eventually, this reform was approved by the General Assembly and the voters in 2002.

Ultimately, the governor argued strongly and later felt like he had privately secured an agreement from Speaker of the House Richards to pass a constitutional amendment giving the governor a two-thirds veto in exchange for agreeing to annual sessions. The veto portion of this arrangement went by the wayside, and despite the success of the Patton administration, this perpetuated the ability of an otherwise strong governor to veto legislation, which may be overridden by the General Assembly with only a 50 percent plus one vote in each chamber.

The rest of this remarkable dinner centered on a discussion on casino gambling, with Governor Jones being strongly in favor. He suggested that it be limited to horse tracks (and not video terminals), which seems to have been prophetic, and thought there should be a constitutional amendment allowing it, as did Governor Brown. Governor Patton favored this, and then Ford and Jones debated hotly whether a constitutional amendment was needed for some time. Governor Patton felt like designated areas of the state, drawing on his economic development experience, that were determined as being economically challenged could be authorized to have casinos, with the proceeds going to the Thoroughbred industry.

Governor Nunn seemed overly concerned about the matter and kept questioning who would run the casinos, with Jones repeatedly coming back to the idea of horse racing, which was his business, and how we must increase purses to draw better horses to the state's racetracks. There were additional prophetic comments from Governors Carroll and Jones about the internet and bringing betting "into the living room" and whether this would hurt or help the tracks. And notably, Governor Nunn zig-zagged a bit during the dinner, raising seemingly disconnected issues such as the need for corporal punishment in public schools.

At one point in the discussion, there was a dialogue on notions to alter state offices enumerated in Kentucky's constitution by either combining them with the governor's executive cabinet, eliminating them or curtailing their responsibilities. Many of the duties of offices, such as the state treasurer or even the secretary of state, had become antiquated. Some thought that economies of scale not only in cost savings but also in public benefit could accrue from having the General Assembly pass legislation putting this reform on a statewide ballot for approval. In a follow-up to this meeting, his general counsel wrote a memorandum to the governor that summarized this initiative discussed among the governors:

To: Governor Patton

From: Denis B. Fleming, Jr.
General Counsel

Date: April 15, 1999

I sent this note to my staff today with copies as indicated to Secretary Luallen, Skipper [Martin] and Jack [Conway] in follow up to our dinner meeting with the former governors:

We need to give careful consideration to precisely whether we can and how we should amend the Kentucky Constitution to provide that the current Offices of Attorney General and State Auditor would be reconstituted such that the elected official can be elected to successive 4-year terms indefinitely but would be prohibited from running for the Office of Governor or Lt. Governor without resigning the office. Relatedly, the Offices of the Commissioner of Agriculture would be eliminated and made an executive office within the Governor's Cabinet and the duties of the Secretary of State would perhaps be merged with those of the Lt. Governor and the Treasurer's Office would be abolished. We need to research and as a product of that research prepare a draft of legislation which would actually contain the ballot language and thereby supersede legislation requiring the Attorney General to prepare such language which is placed on the ballot for approval by the voters after legislative approval. This was done with the Bingo Amendment, so there is factual precedent. In particular, as a precedent we need to consider judicial rules of the Supreme Court which prohibit sitting judges from running for office and look at the provisions in other states which may prohibit inferior constitutional officers from running for higher positions such as Governor and Lt. Governor. Our goal is to have an advanced draft of legislation incorporating valid initiative language for the Governor's consideration and our review with him in early June.[110]

While few of these proposals were placed on the ballot, they were discussed internally within the administration and among leadership of the General Assembly. The notable exception was a constitutional amendment approved by the public allowing the General Assembly to have annual instead of biennial sessions.

The governor's dinner also included discussion on early childhood development and on taxes. Governor Patton felt that if we were forty-second in the nation in per capita income and state taxes "this means we are 42nd in services." Later, he went on to swing for the fence in the year 2000 with one of the major reforms attempted in his second term, which was broad-based tax reform. He spent countless hours preparing the data-based rationale for tax reform, which would have increased the sales tax and taxes on services but lowered other taxes, which would have resulted in $400 million more per year in state revenue.

While Governor Patton was able to get this reform through the Kentucky House and even framed the printout of the favorable House vote on the wall behind his desk, it did not get through the Senate, as he detailed in his memoirs, over a disagreement with Senate president David Williams, a Republican. There was a contentious meeting in the Governor's Mansion with Williams, and there were suggestions of transportation dollars going to certain areas of the state in exchange for enacting tax reform, but all of this derailed in acrimony.

So, what became of this famous dinner? The discussion session in the parlor ended with Governor Patton expressing concern that Kentucky was losing its wealth and was being exploited by out-of-state companies and needed to develop small venture capital initiatives and more venture capital for risky projects. The governor strongly felt that "the transmission of knowledge must be the most important function of society," and he went through a litany of initiatives he later put in place in part, including integrated computer systems in schools, better libraries and investment in state technology. Governor Collins, a former schoolteacher, was very keen on additional technology in the schools and the need for international training and teaching foreign languages, and Governor Brown, the fast-food magnate, innovatively, proposed to establish business schools as incubators to teach entrepreneurship, which was his path to success with Kentucky Fried Chicken and other initiatives prior to becoming governor.

Much of the discussion continued at the large table in the dining room in the Governor's Mansion, with Governor Patton at the head and the governors arranged with the oldest office holders next to him, that being

Breathitt and Nunn, and others around the table in descending order. At one point, Governors Breathitt and Nunn suddenly argued about open housing and public accommodation laws, which Governor Patton had to mediate. This concerned legislation Breathitt supported while governor that Nunn considered overly broad. In Breathitt's administration, Kentucky in 1966 became the first state south of the Mason-Dixon line to enact a public accommodations law.

Toward the end of the dinner, Governor Collins leaned over to a participant and whispered, "What do you think about all this…aren't you glad you came to this dinner?" Her seatmate smiled and said, "Oh yes, Governor, I would not have missed this for anything." Apart from Jefferson's own Commonwealth of Virginia, which gathered nine former governors of that state for a dinner in 1988, this dinner in Kentucky in 1999 was likely the largest gathering of current and former governors of any state in the nation's history.

As to the organizer of this dinner, Paul Patton may have been the most successful governor of Kentucky in the modern era. Not only was he the first governor to have been elected to consecutive terms by the voters, he also came to the job well qualified. Previously, he had been a successful coal operator, served three terms as Pike County judge and was lieutenant governor (1991–95) prior to being elected governor in 1995. Patton was unique in his interest in Kentucky's constitution, the dynamics among the branches of government, and he had ample respect for the judiciary, in part because of the influence of Chief Justice Stephens. He was the first governor, at the invitation of Stephens, to address the Kentucky Supreme Court in person in the Court's Chambers. When he did this, he prepared his remarks carefully and echoed the respect for the judiciary Jefferson encouraged in his work on state constitutions by stressing that each branch of government "is co-equal." Patton enjoyed a good friendship with Stephens, and the two men met often, at times in the Governor's Mansion, to discuss policy matters and constitutional reform.

One topic discussed frequently was an effort to make the judiciary, including the Kentucky Supreme Court, more accountable to the public. While it never surfaced publicly, they discussed whether the state constitution should be amended to provide for a recall of elected judges in the instance of bad behavior or placed on the ballot after six years in their respective districts for a vote of confidence. Neither idea came to fruition, but Jefferson himself might have been proud of Patton's plans for constitutional reform—at one point, Patton even considered the organization of a state constitutional convention.[111]

Chapter 14

RECENT DEVELOPMENTS
IN JEFFERSON'S KENTUCKY LEGACY

LGBTQ+ Rights, the Role of the Press and New Battles Among the Branches of Government

We have seen from more than two hundred years of judicial opinions and political activities that Jefferson's shared concern with John Breckinridge to maintain the independence of the judicial, legislative and executive branches of our state and federal systems was well justified. Jefferson himself, as seen regarding the Louisiana Purchase, was concerned about the extent of his authority as president in 1803 to make this purchase without amending the federal Constitution. He asked Breckinridge to sort it out legislatively and to rely on the treaty clause in the federal Constitution to allow great progress to proceed for the nation. In the modern era, we have seen several governors in Kentucky stretch their authority by executive order, including to propose the implementation of a state budget in an emergency and the use of executive orders in other matters of government construction.

In the spring of 2003, Governor Paul Patton exercised his prerogative as chief executive of Kentucky under Section 81 of the state constitution by signing an order prohibiting discrimination against state government employees or job applicants based on sexual orientation or gender identity. At the time, only twelve states had deployed such an executive order, and while the order was later rescinded by Governor Patton's successor, Governor Fletcher, and was reinstituted immediately by Governors Steve Beshear and his son, Andy Beshear, this order was viewed as a stretch of the governor's constitutional authority. Patton was quoted as believing that the action "was the right thing to do" and structured it as applying to the governor's executive cabinet agencies, which at the time employed more than thirty thousand people.

While the order made it a policy of Kentucky not to discriminate on any of several bases—including race, religion, sex, age or disability in accord with federal law—sexual orientation and gender identity were the key additions suggested to Governor Patton by then state senator and now judge Ernesto Scorsone of Lexington. The policy was akin to those in "fairness ordinances" that contained similar language enacted by local municipalities such as Louisville, Lexington and Covington. Although the order did not apply to public institutions or agencies under the governor's direct control, such as school districts, colleges and universities, it put the state's executive branch on notice that there was to be no discrimination in hiring or pay and no harassment of individuals for the stated reasons, including sexual orientation or gender identity.

The order was groundbreaking and received a great deal of national press. In his press release with the order, Governor Patton reiterated "the philosophy of this administration which establishes as state policy the principle that people should be judged by their qualifications and conduct in the workplace and not by their status." Patton went on to state that the order intended to "provide equal employment opportunity to all people in all aspects of employer-employee relations."[112]

By this time, it was the end of the Patton administration, and the governor requested his general counsel prepare a memorandum for him providing assurances to him as to the legal underpinnings of his proposed groundbreaking executive order. This memorandum is exemplary of the detail this governor was interested in from a constitutional perspective, and in terms of legal precedent, to proceed as he intended. Dated April 2003, the order was issued one month later and cited the governor's authority as chief executive under Kentucky's constitution permitting him to stretch his authority, as governors and even presidents have done under the federal Constitution:

Memorandum
To: Governor Paul Patton
From: Denis Fleming
Date: April 1, 2003
Re: Executive Order Prohibiting Discrimination in Employment

As you know, Senator Scorsone has asked you to issue an Executive Order prohibiting discrimination in state employment practices based upon sexual orientation. In many ways, Kentucky has been at the forefront of addressing matters of sexual orientation with the enactment of its hate crimes legislation in 1998 and in particular with the groundbreaking decision of the Kentucky Supreme Court in Commonwealth vs. Wasson in 1993 (opinion attached Exhibit A). This was a decision which held that a Kentucky criminal statute proscribing consensual homosexual sodomy violated the privacy and equal protection guarantees of the Kentucky Constitution.

In recent years, the Governors of 13 states have issued Executive Orders which prohibit discrimination based upon sexual orientation in public employment only. (Executive Orders attached Exhibit B). These states include Indiana (most recently issued by Governor O'Bannon), Illinois, Louisiana, Maryland, Michigan, Minnesota, New Mexico, New York, Ohio, Pennsylvania, Rhode Island and Washington State. In addition, 8 states and the District of Columbia have passed statutes banning discrimination on the basis of sexual orientation in public and private employment and private sector discrimination is prohibited in many counties and cities and at least 71 cities and counties have gay anti-bias laws (including Louisville's Fairness Ordinance and the City of Lexington, KY).

Should you consider the issuance of such an Executive Order in the remainder of your term there are a variety of ways the issue can be addressed. For example, as in the case of Governor O'Bannon, you could simply establish a policy to provide equal employment opportunity to employees in all aspects of employee/employer relations without discrimination because of race, color, religion, sex, national origin, sexual orientation, ancestry, age, disability, or veteran status. Governor O'Bannon likewise included language expressing the intent of state government to maintain a working environment free of "sexual harassment and intimidation."

Why would Kentucky need such an Executive Order applicable to state government? Studies have shown sexual orientation discrimination takes many forms and is often underreported or never reported at all. Anecdotal evidence indicates that gay men and lesbians are often denied jobs, promotions and security based upon their sexual orientation. The armed forces age old ban of gay men and lesbians has led to successful legal challenges by officers discharged because of their sexual preferences and to political efforts to repeal the policy entirely. Meinhold vs. U.S. Department of Defense (C.D. Cal. 1993). Pruitt vs. Cheney 963 F. 2nd 1190 (9th Cir. 1991). Some law enforcement agencies have used their state sodomy statutes to effectively ban gay men and lesbians, yet these policies are eroding under challenge and were eliminated in Kentucky with the Wasson decision in

1993. The forceful argument causing this rethinking is that people should be judged by their conduct in the workplace, not by their status.

Ideally, government employers should not discriminate against employees based on sexual orientation on the theory that governments are subject to constitutional requirements that they act fairly and rationally toward all citizens including employees. In some situations, gay and lesbian employees may claim due process and equal protection rights under the 5th and 14th amendments to the United States Constitution as well as under Sections 1 and 2 of Kentucky's Constitution. However, at present no federal law exists which protects individuals based on sexual orientation. Title VII of the Civil Rights Act of 1964 forbids discrimination in employment based on race, color, religion, national origin and sex. It has been consistently held that the Title VII prohibition against discrimination based on sex does not include sexual orientation; the ban on sex discrimination covers practices based on gender, not sexual practices and preferences. Plattner vs. Cash and Thomas Contractors, Inc. 908 F. 2nd 902 (11th Cir. 1990). Similarly, it is clear that neither Title VII nor the Americans with Disabilities Act cover discrimination against transsexuals or bisexuals or against a male because he is effeminate. Smith vs. Liberty Mutual Insurance Company 395 F. Supp. 1098 (N.D. GA. 1975). Although numerous bills have been introduced in Congress to outlaw discrimination based on sexual orientation none has passed. However, the United States Supreme Court recently agreed to consider, and heard oral arguments last week, in a Texas case which challenges that states criminal sodomy laws on equal protection and privacy grounds. It is expected that the Supreme Court may reverse its previous position and recognize a constitutionally grounded right to privacy among gays and lesbians.

Senator Scorsone has forwarded to you for review polling data which indicates that in Louisville and Lexington over 70% of registered voters polled in Louisville believe it should be illegal to fire someone because of their sexual orientation or to refuse to rent an apartment to a person because of their sexual orientation (Exhibit C). It should be noted that you signed an Affirmative Action Plan May 15, 1996, on behalf of state government which secured or committed the state to secure for all Kentuckians "equal employment opportunities and freedom from discrimination and other forms of harassment, including sexual harassment because of race, color, religion, national origin, disability, sex or age" but sexual orientation was not included. (Executive Order 96-612—May 15, 1996 Exhibit D). Although an Executive Order to the effect requested would garner publicity in Kentucky, I believe an Order could be reasonably crafted which would prohibit non-discriminatory employment practices in a variety of areas. Perhaps such an Order could be part of your efforts to respond to the disparity study recently released regarding state contracting for minorities. I would urge you to read the Wasson decision of the Kentucky Supreme Court to understand the state of the criminal law in Kentucky which has been in place now for over 10 years. Senator Scorsone successfully represented the Plaintiff in this case before the Ky. Supreme Court. As U.S. Supreme Court Justice Harry A. Blackmun wrote in his dissent from a ruling upholding Georgia's sodomy statute (the majority opinion for which most likely will be overruled in the near future):

> *Only the most willful blindness could obscure the fact that sexual intimacy is a sensitive, key relationship of human nature, central to family life, community welfare and the development of human personality. The fact that individuals define themselves in a significant way through their intimate sexual relationships with others suggests, in a Nation as diverse as ours, that there may be many "right" ways of conducting those relationships and that much of the richness of a relationship will come from the freedom an individual has to choose the form and nature of these intensely personal bonds. (Bowers vs. Hardwick 478 US 186, 205 (1986).*

> *Attached as Exhibit E are two versions of an executive order which have been prepared by Senator Scorsone. These drafts are an excellent starting point, but I would suggest they be revised along the lines of some of the other orders attached from other states should you choose to issue such an order during your term.*[113]

In subsequent years, the fate of this landmark executive order was innately partisan. In the administration of Governor Fletcher from 2004 to 2007, the order issued by Governor Patton was immediately rescinded. Later, in the administrations of Governor Steve Beshear and his son, Andy Beshear, who is the current governor of Kentucky, the order was revised and reissued. Also, in 2004, during the Fletcher administration, the Kentucky General Assembly passed and the state approved an amendment to Kentucky's constitution stating that marriage in the Commonwealth is only between a man and a woman.

By the time the U.S. Supreme Court took up this matter in 2014, thirty-one states had provisions in their state constitutions placing a ban on same-sex marriage. These state laws would be overturned on equal protection and other grounds under our federal Constitution by the Supreme Court in 2015 in the landmark Supreme Court decision *Obergefell v. Hodges*. This decision was a blockbuster event for the LGBTQ+ community and the nation when the Supreme Court ruled that same-sex couples in the United States have the same right to marry as different-sex couples regardless of their state of residence.

It is important to include a note on the valuable role the Kentucky and national press corps has played in the advancement of public policy, constitutional reform and the betterment of government. "Good government" is an amorphous phrase, but to many experienced in state and federal government, it is something that tends to come about thanks to the critical role of print and often television journalism and radio reportage. Few if any of the reforms, including constitutional amendments, are achieved without the active support of or at the instigation of the press and good reporting.

During their time in public service, Thomas Jefferson and John Breckinridge certainly were cerebral and focused on details of the law, but both had respect for the role of the press. In a lengthy letter from Jefferson to fellow Virginian Edward Carrington in January 1787, Jefferson detailed his views in favor of an open and vigorous press. Carrington was a Revolutionary War hero, confidant of George Washington, an attorney and attended the Continental Congress in 1786 as a delegate from Virginia. In his letter to Carrington, Jefferson stated:

> *The basis of our governments being the opinion of the people, the very first object should be to keep that right; And were it left to me to decide whether we should have a government without newspapers or newspapers without a government, I should not hesitate a moment to prefer the latter.*[114]

In the modern era, Governor Patton deserves credit not only for promoting constitutional reform and encouraging annual legislative sessions and a merged city-county government but also for higher education reform he worked to achieve with great success. This was a landmark reform that established the Council on Post-Secondary Education for higher education planning and policy development; established the Kentucky Community and Technical College System, which combined these systems; and deleted the University of Kentucky's authority over the degree-granting coordination of community colleges. The reform also established a matching fund for endowed scholarships at Kentucky's major universities, later known as "Bucks for Brains." This program was expanded to provide all major public universities with matching grants in medical and dental fields, criminal justice reform, technical and service industries and a host of other initiatives. It is now in its twenty-fifth year of success in Kentucky and has been duplicated in other states.

The role of the press was critical to the success of this reform, which continues to pay enormous dividends to Kentucky. The work particularly of the *Louisville Courier-Journal*, the *Lexington Herald-Leader* and even Kentucky's rural newspapers, be they weekly or otherwise, cannot be underestimated. David Hawpe, the editor of the *Courier-Journal*, and editor Keith Runyon played a critical role in the support of higher education reform. They encouraged good reporting and more often used the editorial page of that paper to support this reform, including decoupling of the community college and technical college system from the University of Kentucky, the university from which Hawpe, the governor and others in public service were alumni.

Reporters of this Louisville newspaper, including Al Cross, Tom Loftus, Deborah Yetter and Joe Gerth, along with Bill Estep, Jack Brammer and Jamie Luke and others of the *Lexington Herald Leader* and other city and regional papers combined to keep policy makers on their toes. This was not only on critical legislation dealing with higher education, criminal justice reform and coal mine safety, but they would not hesitate to take people to task as well. This included matters of ethics, be they perceived or actual conflicts of interest, Kentucky Derby tickets or the use of economic development incentives grants to counties or travel expenses. They helped public servants be better stewards of the public interest.

Good advice to those in public service or who wish to pursue a career in this field is that a policy of openness and cooperation as opposed to confrontation with the press is better not only for yourself but also for the officeholder whom you serve. This attitude, more importantly, can result in a better policy outcome for the state and its citizens. The press and individual reporters have a job to do, and while discretion and confidentiality are often mandated by a circumstance such as a pending appointment, a major corporation locating a plant in the state or even a pending investigation or criminal matter, as a rule one is better served being transparent with the press whenever possible.

When R.G. Dunlop with the *Courier-Journal*, an excellent investigative and Peabody Award–winning reporter, ran a series of stories challenging Governor Patton's mine safety record when he was in this business, he was surely annoyed by it. But to his credit, he took it upon himself to develop legislation addressing the matters raised in the articles, resulting in a material improvement in the safety of coal miners on the job in Kentucky. The governor likewise deserved credit for appointing to a state position a chief critic and lawyer for the mine workers community, Tony Oppegard, to oversee mine safety.

Occasionally, an officeholder would get an unexpected compliment from the press. In the spring of 2000, during a regular session of the General Assembly, House Bill 70, sponsored by Representative Tom Kerr, sought to exclude church camps and other religious-related facilities from Kentucky's civil rights laws. The bill passed the House by a vote of 82-17 and then passed the Senate 17-12. Governor Patton held the bill two weeks before vetoing it on March 8, the day it would have become law with or without his signature. Supporters of the bill viewed it as a religious freedom issue, while opponents voiced concerns over limiting civil rights.

In his veto message, Patton noted that religious organizations are not required to open their facilities to the public. Religious groups that do rent their facilities to the public "must obey the same laws that non-religious entities are required to obey." He said that HB 70 "violates both the spirit and the meaning of the Kentucky Civil Rights Acts by permitting discrimination on the basic of religion." Regrettably, Kentucky's constitution provides the legislature may override a veto of the governor with a majority vote in both chambers, which took place in this instance.

This weak veto power in Kentucky's constitution, being one of only six states that does not require a two-thirds vote to override a governor's veto, was a limitation on the power of the executive Jefferson may have been concerned with.[115] One area of agreement among Jefferson as well as the authors of *The Federalist Papers* was the check on the power of the legislature that an executive veto carried with it. But in this instance, Governor Patton was pleased to see an editorial in the *Courier-Journal* after his veto message that complimented the governor's action with a photo of him and the headline "Governor Patton: Vetoing Discrimination."[116]

The press in Kentucky continues to do an admirable job covering the ever-changing notions of the General Assembly to add additional provisions to Kentucky's constitution. The separation of powers clauses in Kentucky's first constitutions remain in the present version. Kentucky has had four state constitutions, with the current constitution being adopted in 1891 with a preamble and twenty articles contained in a lengthy document. Unlike the infrequent amendments to our federal Constitution, the current Kentucky Constitution has been amended forty times.

Recent amendments to Kentucky's constitution have focused on detailed policy issues, with one of the last amendments approved by the voters occurring in 2020. This was when Amendment 1, known as the Marcy's Law Crime Victims Compensation Rights Amendment, was passed. This measure provided crime victims with constitutional rights, including the right to be treated with due consideration for victim safety and dignity, the right to be notified about the release or escape of a person accused or convicted of committing a crime against them and for restitution from an individual who committed a criminal offense. Recently, the constitutional amendment mentioned earlier to limit the governor's pardon power has cleared a state Senate Committee. This amendment was proposed in response to the perceived abuses of Governor Matt Bevin in his use of the pardon power during his administration.

Again, the press played a pivotal role in setting the stage for this amendment. In a lengthy series of articles, the *Louisville Courier-Journal* exposed the pardon processes of the Bevin administration as allegedly violating legal norms, highlighting racial disparities. Most recently, Kentucky's General Assembly passed a constitutional amendment to be placed on the ballot banning noncitizen voting. Even though the Kentucky Constitution provides that every citizen of the United States with Kentucky residency is eligible to vote in the state's elections, many lawmakers felt that the wording required more specificity.

The federal Constitution has a specific prohibition against noncitizen voting, and this proposed amendment in Kentucky would focus on a prohibition against municipalities allowing noncitizens to vote in local elections. As of 2024, the Kentucky General Assembly has under consideration twenty constitutional amendments, of which two have been placed by law on the November ballot for approval by the public after passage by each chamber of the legislature by 60 percent or more.

A notable coda to the supposed controversy as to whether Jefferson had any involvement in Kentucky's constitution is a remarkable 333-page split decision with a lengthy dissent in the Kentucky Court of Appeals case *Schell et al. v. Beshear et al.*, March 8, 2024. This opinion reaches a seemingly correct decision over its first 41 pages as to the unconstitutionality of an appointment by the legislature of ex-officio members to the Kentucky Fair Board, which was challenged by Governor Andy Beshear. Indeed, the majority opinion relies on Sections 27 and 28, the separation of powers provisions in Kentucky's constitution saying for the General Assembly to appoint themselves ex-officio, nonvoting members of the State Fair

Board, "crosses the boundaries established by Secs. 27 and 28 of the Kentucky Constitution."[117]

On page 144, however, as part of the dissent to the holding, there is an effort to refute the notion of Jefferson's involvement with Kentucky's constitution, much less any suggestion by Jefferson for the inclusion of separation of powers clauses in that document. At one point, the dissent suggests that Jefferson's involvement story in Kentucky's constitution is "a hoax." The dissent goes on to suggest that George Nicholas and Thomas Jefferson essentially despised each other, citing, among other things, a supposed overcharge of legal expenses by Nicholas against Jefferson. It then states that "any relationship" of John Breckinridge and Jefferson before 1790 was unlikely, though admitting that a relationship between Jefferson and Breckinridge "may have begun as early as 1796."

As we have seen, these gentlemen served together in Virginia as early as 1780, when Nicholas and Breckinridge were members of the Virginia House of Delegates, when Jefferson himself was governor of Virginia having been elected in 1779. Correspondence of Jefferson at the time is complimentary of the work of Nicholas in the Virginia House of Delegates in the 1780s, saying that Nicholas was a "very honest and able man," casting doubt on the suggestion that Nicholas did not "darken the door" of Jefferson by 1790 and that "not until 1798…did Jefferson have anything kind to say about Nicholas." Beginning in 1780 and for many years after, as evidenced by his handwritten correspondence, Nicholas lived in Charlottesville, Virginia, less than four miles from Monticello.

Further, the assertion in the dissent that "nothing indicates Nicholas had any role in a specific separation of powers provision" seems in doubt from repeated handwritten references to Jefferson in the notes of Nicholas for the 1792 Kentucky Constitutional Convention. As stated, a page of the Nicholas Papers deals directly with separation of powers doctrine and includes a reference to page 195 of Jefferson's *Notes on the State of Virginia* dealing with this very topic. Another folder from these handwritten papers for over 8 pages discusses the need for barriers among the branches of government, again referencing "Jefferson" at the end with a citation to his writings on government structure. We have seen in the third chapter that Jefferson is cited repeatedly by name in the Nicholas Papers in support of the need to establish separation among the branches of government as eventually set forth in Kentucky's constitution. Likewise, the cited works of Kentucky historians support the early interaction between Nicholas and Jefferson and their friendship, as well as with Breckinridge, long before the 1792 convention.

Left: Portrait of Thomas Jefferson in 1821 at age seventy-eight. Painted at Monticello by Thomas Scully. *Thomas Jefferson Foundation, public domain.*

Below: Paul Patton, governor of Kentucky from 1995 to 2003 (middle right), with other Kentucky governors in 1999. Patton was also lieutenant governor of Kentucky, Pike County judge executive and president of the University of Pikeville. *Photo in possession of the author.*

Nicholas and his brothers Cary and John Nicholas were longtime associates of Jefferson beginning as early as 1780 in Virginia. Indeed, the brother-in-law of Nicholas went on to serve as secretary of the navy in Jefferson's cabinet. Cary Nicholas, later governor of Virginia (1814–16) and U.S. senator from Virginia (1799–1804), lived on Tufton Farm, less than a mile from Monticello and on property owned by Jefferson. Prior to this, he lived on his farm near Warren, Virginia, less than twenty miles from Monticello. His daughter, Jane Nicholas, married Thomas Jefferson Randolph, the eldest grandson of Jefferson. Cary Nicholas died at Tufton Farm in 1820 and is buried at the Monticello Cemetery.[118]

Finally, the dissent in *Schell* states that the federal Constitution is "a document Jefferson took no part in drafting" (page 144). While Jefferson at the time of the 1787 constitutional convention was overseas as minister to France, by his own admission in a letter written from Monticello to George Washington in 1792, he wrote several letters, "not half a dozen," to participants in the convention with detailed proposals for the document, some of which were included.[119]

Jefferson appears to have been a firm believer in the natural evolution of a constitution, be it federal or state. In a letter to James Madison written from Paris shortly after the beginning of the French Revolution in 1789, he proposed, "Every constitution then, and every law naturally expires at the end of 19 years. If it be enforced longer, it is an act of force and not of right."

In other words, he supported the notion that each generation has the right to examine its state or federal constitution and make changes subject to public approval. He continued to believe this principle throughout his life, and in a letter to a colleague in 1816, he wrote with disapproval, "Some men look at constitutions with sanctimonious reverence and deemed them like the ark of the covenant, too sacred to be touched." Jefferson was clearly not of this view.[120]

CONCLUSION

Late in life, at age seventy-nine, Jefferson wrote a letter to his longtime friend Spencer Roane, who was a distinguished Virginia lawyer and judge on the Supreme Court of Virginia for twenty-seven years. Roane would correspond sporadically with Jefferson, posing several topics for his consideration. Roane was a prodigy of sorts, having been admitted to study law at William & Mary when he was fourteen, admitted to practice law at twenty and served in the Virginia House of Delegates shortly after Jefferson was governor. Apparently in one of these letters to Jefferson, he inquired as to the proper exercise of the three branches of government under a constitutional system. Jefferson replied to Roane on September 6, 1819, from Poplar Forest, his modest but beautiful retreat in rural Virginia near Lynchburg about sixty miles from Monticello:

> *Each of the three departments has equally the right to decide for itself what is its duty under the constitution, without any regard to what the others may have decided for themselves under a similar question. But you intimate a wish that my opinion should be known on this subject. No dear Sir. I withdraw from all contests of opinion and resign everything cheerfully to the generation now in place.*[121]

This reply may suggest a state of honest exhaustion on the topic, but it's remarkable that Jefferson still seems to be addressing the subject of his focus more than thirty years after his work on the Virginia and Kentucky Constitutions.

Jefferson's close friendship with John Breckinridge; his work reforming the penal code of Virginia, which Breckinridge carried into Kentucky law; his writing of the Kentucky Resolutions; and, most likely, the separation of powers clauses in the Virginia and Kentucky Constitutions all favor his influence on Kentucky politics and these documents. Certainly, as we have seen, the Kentucky Supreme Court took great pains to detail the uniqueness of Kentucky's separation of powers clauses and Jefferson's direct involvement in them. On four occasions, the Court declared that Jefferson contributed clauses Sections 27 and 28 to Kentucky's constitution. And from extensive handwritten notes in his papers on the 1792 Kentucky Constitution, it seems that the father of that constitution, George Nicholas, had Jefferson in mind, with repeated direct references to Jefferson when he and others prepared a separation of powers article for this document.

Whether the meeting alleged to have taken place in 1792 at Monticello between Jefferson, Breckinridge and Nicholas on Kentucky's constitution indeed happened remains to be determined. We know that Nicholas lived just miles from Jefferson starting in 1780, when he moved from Williamsburg to Charlottesville while Nicholas was serving in the Virginia House of Delegates and Jefferson was governor of Virginia. Breckinridge as well traveled this territory between Virginia and Kentucky often and served in the Virginia House of Delegates when Jefferson was governor. He must certainly have associated with Jefferson on matters of government and substance and likewise lived near Jefferson and Virginia's capitals of Richmond and, temporarily, Williamsburg.

Further, we have seen Jefferson operate furtively at times. He secretly authored the Kentucky Resolutions, which he acknowledged he did privately in a letter to Madison and later in 1821 in correspondence to James Breckinridge. The Jefferson scholar Dumas Malone suggests that Cary Nicholas, brother of George Nicholas, may have been the conduit of the Kentucky Resolutions, written by Jefferson for delivery to Breckinridge, who sponsored them in the Kentucky General Assembly. Jefferson likewise is observed supporting the 1801 Judiciary Act but later having Congress repeal portions he felt were used improperly to expand the federal court system for political reasons. He also was preparing legislation as president and showing it to Breckinridge for his thoughts while Breckinridge was attorney general right up until Breckinridge died in 1806. Given this wealth of stealthy circumstances, it's just as likely as not that the alleged meeting at Monticello in 1792 took place or perhaps some form of it occurred.

While Jefferson may have been frustrated with the inability to include separation of powers clauses in the federal Constitution, as evidenced by Madison's polite refusal of the notion in *The Federalist Papers*, it is notable in 1787 during the time of the constitutional convention that John Adams and Thomas Jefferson were simply not around. Both were serving as American ministers abroad in France and Great Britain, respectively, at the time of the constitutional convention. Had Jefferson been there, the results may have been different. But for our purposes, there can be no doubt that these clauses, through repeated judicial interpretation by Kentucky's Supreme Court, have been used effectively to validate many of the great policy reforms in Kentucky's history. While all these events happened long ago, we may all thank Jefferson for his work and the legacy he left us.

NOTES

Foreword

1. Justice George DuRelle of the Kentucky Supreme Court (then called the Kentucky Court of Appeals) dissenting in the Court's decision *Commissioners of Sinking Fund v. George* (1898); Justice William Cooper in his opinion for the Kentucky Supreme Court in *Fletcher v. Office of the Attorney General ex rel. Stumbo*, n3 (2005), Judge Glenn E. Acree dissenting to the decision of the Kentucky Court of Appeals in *Schell et al. v. Beshear et al.* (2024).

Chapter 3

2. Article IV, Section 4 of the Virginia Constitution provides, in part, "Any person may be elected to the House of Delegates who, at the time of the election, is twenty-one years of age, is a resident of the house district which he is seeking to represent and is qualified to vote for members of the General Assembly."
3. Harrison, "John Breckinridge," 9.
4. Daniel Boone, notable frontiersman and early settler of Kentucky, at age forty-seven was likewise elected to Virginia's House of Delegates in 1781 and served in this body with Breckinridge, Patrick Henry, George Nicholas (a future attorney general of Kentucky), Benjamin Harrison (father of future president William Henry Harrison), Benjamin Logan

(a future member of the Kentucky General Assembly and candidate for governor) and John Tyler Sr. (father of future governor of Virginia and president John Tyler).

5. Rules of the Constitutional Society of Virginia, June 14, 1784.

6. Nicholas was keenly attuned to military matters and an early supporter of the aims of the American Revolutionary War. He served as an officer in the Virginia regiment beginning in 1775 when he was twenty-one, rising to the rank of lieutenant colonel in 1777. His family appears to have referred to him as "Colonel Nicholas," as did others in contemporary correspondence. Historical Marker 125 near his grave at the Old Episcopal Third Street Cemetery on East Third Street in Lexington, Kentucky, refers to him as "Colonel George Nicholas" and "Father of the Kentucky Constitution."

7. See the biographical sketch of George Nicholas and handwritten correspondence of Nicholas during this period in which he notes that he is in Charlottesville, both in the Reuben T. Durrett Collection of the George Nicholas Papers in the Hanna Holborn Gray Special Collections Research Center, University of Chicago Library, Series II—Correspondence of Nicholas, Box 1, Folders 2 and 3. Jefferson in 1792 was secretary of state, serving under President George Washington and living intermittently at Monticello outside Charlottesville. The U.S. capital in 1792 was Philadelphia but was in the process of being moved to Washington, D.C., a location closer to native Virginians like Washington, Jefferson and Madison.

8. George Nicholas to Wilson Cary Nicholas, May 8, 1789, Albert and Shirley Small Special Collections Repository, University of Virginia, Papers of Wilson Cary Nicholas, Box 1, Folder 26.

9. Nicholas corresponded often with Madison, a Federalist, from 1788 to 1790, as did Kentuckian and later U.S. senator from Kentucky John Brown (1757–1837), at one point asking Madison for "some remarks upon Jefferson's plan of government denoting such alterations as would render it more applicable to the District of Kentucky." The "plan of government" was the draft constitution for Virginia that Jefferson had prepared in 1783 and later included in Jefferson's *Notes on Virginia*, discussed infra, which included decided preferences for a distinct separation of powers provision. Kentucky's statehood, however, was not granted until 1792, with the state constitution adopted by the convention that year bearing more influence from Jefferson than Madison.

10. Dupre, "Political Ideas of George Nicholas," 201–5.

11. Ibid., 201–3. Dupre likewise on these pages references a letter from Madison to Jefferson, at that time minister to France, complimenting the intellect and hard work of Nicholas.

12. In a second letter to his brother Cary in November 1789, George Nicholas was again uncertain of federal office, declaring that he would not accept the appointment of President Washington "if it is an obstacle" to anything "he can make a profit from" and would not accept public office without a salary. Despite these misgivings, he accepted the office. Albert and Shirley Small Special Collections Library, Wilson Cary Nicholas Papers, Box 1, Folder 29.

13. Reuben Durrett (1824–1913) was a Louisville, Kentucky attorney, historian and at one point editor of the *Louisville Courier* newspaper. In his retirement from the practice of law, he worked on preserving records of Kentucky's history and collected thousands of books, historical letters and manuscripts. In 1913, shortly before his death, Durrett's family finalized the sale of Durrett's papers to the University of Chicago. This sale included the papers Durrett had collected concerning George Nicholas. In 1884, he and nine others in Louisville founded the Filson Cub, now known as the Filson Historical Society.

14. Harrison, "John Breckinridge," 30–39.

15. Still more references to "Jefferson" appear in the Nicholas Papers, apparently in the handwriting of Nicholas and on the last two pages in a different folder (Box 1, Folder 15) that is undated and labeled "Expenses, land taxes, loan office and Jefferson." The first reference to Jefferson on the next to last page of the folder states, "Adams 176. Jefferson 158." Then the last or what may be the back of another page states, "Expenses of Government, Land taxes, loan office Jefferson." The meaning of these references is conjecture. The content of this folder is ten pages, and while at times difficult to read, it appears to concern the finances of a government, with the first sentence of the first page in the hand of Nicholas beginning, "The expenses of government may be divided into two types…."

16. Tauber, "Notes on the State of Virginia," 635–48; see page 646 for discussion of page 126 of Jefferson's *Notes*.

17. Nicholas Papers, University of Chicago Library, Box 1, Folder 25, "Speech—Speech in Kentucky Convention (circa 1792)," 1–8.

18. Nicholas Papers, Box 1, Folder 31, of an eighty-seven-page handwritten treatise where on page 12 is referenced Montesquieu and Jefferson in an essay on governmental powers and "the purposes of establishing different houses of representation."

19. Nicholas appears from correspondence to be complaining of health problems shortly before his death on June 22, 1799, at age forty-five. He was described as "of a stocky build, large head, almost entirely bald and vey overweight." His friend James Madison, upon being shown a caricature of Nicholas in 1788, purportedly "laughed until he cried" when someone compared his appearance to "a bowl of plum pudding with legs on it." Gies, "Kentucky's First Statesman."

20. "First Constitution for the State of Kentucky, 1792, Danville, Kentucky," Kentucky Secretary of State, History Section, https://www.sos.ky.gov/Pages/default.aspx.

21. The lineage of this case law in Kentucky Supreme Court decisions is discussed in the ninth chapter, with the dissenting opinion of Justice Durelle in *Commissioners of Sinking Fund v. George* (1898) having the most detailed description of the purported meeting of Breckinridge and Nicholas with Jefferson at Monticello in 1792.

22. Harrison, "John Breckinridge," 38.

23. The books Breckinridge packed for the journey included thirteen volumes of *Debates in Parliament*, ten volumes of Shakespeare, Plutarch's *Lives*, Locke's *On Government*, Cicero's *Orations*, Gibbon's *Roman Empire*, Milton's *Paradise Lost*, Hume's *History of England* and Adam Smith's *Wealth of Nations*.

24. Lowell Harrison in his excellent biography, "John Breckinridge: Jeffersonian Republican," indicates that Native Americans as late as 1793 often would place a settler captive on a riverbank pleading for help, only for the riverboat travelers to find themselves victims of an attack once they reached shore.

25. A nineteenth-century photo of what purportedly is the law office of Breckinridge at Cabell's Dale is seen in the fourth chapter of this book.

26. Harrison, "John Breckinridge," 51.

27. Shelby was particularly tenacious at the victorious Battle of Kings Mountain, fought near the end of the Revolutionary War. Shelby led Patriot militia against Loyalist militia in repeated charges up a great oval-shaped hill in present-day rural northwest South Carolina in October 1780. Shelby's band of 240 mountain men joined militia from other states in this desperate battle that Thomas Jefferson later described as "the turn of the tide of success" in the entire war. For a good account of Shelby's exploits leading militiamen in this battle, see Dunkerly, *Battle of Kings Mountain*.

Chapter 4

28. High Federalists were a faction of the Federalist Party of John Adams largely led by Alexander Hamilton. They came to fore late in the term of President Adams around 1800, when they broke with Adams over his refusal to widen the undeclared naval war already underway with France in the Caribbean. This fracture within the Federalist Party led to its demise shortly after the election of Jefferson as president in 1801.

29. The Democratic-Republican Party, founded by Jefferson and James Madison, was a political party notable for its support of westward expansion, strict limits on the national government and relative social and political equality. The party tended to oppose centralized government ideas such as a national bank and saw the opposing Federalist Party, led in part by John Adams, as being aristocratic and divisive. The Federalist Party began to wane after Jefferson's election as president in 1800, and the Democratic-Republican Party had all but collapsed by 1830.

30. Clay had a remarkable career as a member of the U.S. House of Representatives from Kentucky, Speaker of the House, U.S. senator from Kentucky and secretary of state during the administration of President John Quincy Adams. He was three times an unsuccessful candidate for president. Other than the Tariff of 1833, his notable achievements included helping to manage the addition of new states into the Union by leading passage of the Missouri Compromise in 1820 and the Compromise of 1850, done largely by finessing issues related to enslavement.

31. In 1799, shortly before his death, George Nicholas published in Lexington and later reprinted in Philadelphia a thirty-nine-page letter from himself to "His Friend in Virginia Justifying the Conduct of the Citizens of Kentucky, As to Some Late Measures of the General Government." The letter concerned the Kentucky Resolutions and constituted a defense of these proposals in the face of opposition by other states of the approach. Jefferson's anonymity was preserved in the letter, but it demonstrates the close connections of Jefferson with Nicholas and Breckinridge, who sponsored the Resolutions in the Kentucky General Assembly. Jefferson was so pleased with the logic of his close friend Nicholas that he wrote to Archibald Stuart in 1799 urging the distribution of the pamphlet in Virginia in support of that state's version of the Kentucky Resolutions. Malone, *Jefferson and His Time*, 3:412–15.

32. *Kentucky Gazette*, November 15, 1798, Lexington, Kentucky Public Library Online Digital Collection.

33. Incredibly, Livingston set a near record in government tenure, as he went on to serve as U.S. attorney for New York, mayor of New York City, congressman and, later, senator from Louisiana, secretary of state and finally ambassador to France under President Andrew Jackson. While in Louisiana, he authored the Livingston Code, a new code of criminal law and procedure widely adopted in European countries. Sir Henry Maine, the prominent British jurist, called Livingston "the first legal genius of modern times."

34. *Kentucky Gazette*, August 15, 1798, 2, Lexington Kentucky Public Library Online Digital Collection.

35. Heidler and Heidler, *Henry Clay*, 27–31.

36. Letter of Jefferson to John Taylor, June 4, 1798, National Archives Founders Online Digital Collection.

37. See Cecere, *Invasion of Virginia*.

38. For a lively treatment of this subject regarding reportage in the *Kentucky Gazette* on the French Revolution in the eighteenth century, see Dupre, "Kentucky Gazette Reports the French Revolution."

39. *Journal of the Kentucky House of Representatives* (November 8, 1798): 3–8.

Chapter 5

40. Dumas, *Jefferson and His Time*, 1:398–409.

41. Thomas Jefferson to Wilson Cary Nicholas, October 5, 1798, in Ford, *Works of Thomas Jefferson*.

42. Ibid.

43. Thomas Jefferson to Wilson Cary Nicholas, September 5, 1799, in Ford, *Works of Thomas Jefferson*.

44. Dumas, *Jefferson and His Time*, 1:406.

45. Thomas Jefferson to John Breckinridge, January 29, 1800, Philadelphia, National Archives Founders Online Digital Collection.

46. Also notable is the groundbreaking case of the U.S. Supreme Court on the First Amendment, *New York Times v. Sullivan* (1964), which referenced this subject, stating that "although the Sedition Act was never tested in this Court, the attack upon its validity has carried the day in the court of history."

Chapter 6

47. Harrison, "John Breckinridge and the Kentucky Constitution of 1799."

48. The direct election of U.S. senators by popular vote was established in the Seventeenth Amendment to the U.S. Constitution, which was ratified by the states in 1913.

49. Kentucky's General Assembly in December 1802 condemned the action of Spain in revoking the right of deposit in New Orleans and transmitted the resolution to Breckinridge through Governor Garrard for presentation to Jefferson. *Kentucky Gazette*, December 7, 1802.

50. By this time in 1803, Cary Nicholas, the brother of George Nicholas, was serving as U.S. senator from Virginia (1799–1804) and was privately advising Jefferson on ways to effectuate the Louisiana Purchase without amending the federal Constitution. In a letter to Nicholas from Monticello written on September 7, 1803, just weeks after his letter to Breckinridge on this topic, Jefferson took issue with the suggestion of Nicholas that he could act unilaterally on the purchase. Recognizing to Nicholas "the force of the arguments you make on the power given by the Constitution to Congress to admit new states into the Union" he thought that "the limits of the U.S. are precisely fixed by the Treaty of 1783" and stated, "I do not believe it was meant that they might receive England, Ireland, Holland etc. into it." From Thomas Jefferson to Wilson Cary Nicholas, Monticello, September 7, 1803, National Archives Founders Online Digital Collection.

51. President Thomas Jefferson to John Breckinridge, August 12, 1803, Monticello, National Archives Founders Online Digital Collection.

52. A critical motivation of Breckinridge, if not Jefferson and the nation, in moving forward with the Louisiana Purchase was the importance of access to the Mississippi River, including to Kentucky. The Spanish and French had periodically blocked access to the Gulf of Mexico, which was devastating economically to those states along the Mississippi and led to political problems. This purchase in part resolved this significant national security issue for the United States.

53. National Archives Founders Online Digital Collection.

54. *American Insurance Company v. Canter*, 26 U.S. 511, U.S. Supreme Court, 1828.

55. President Thomas Jefferson to John Breckinridge, August 7, 1805, Monticello, National Archives Founders Online Digital Collection.

56. Harrison, "John Breckinridge," 192. Albert Gallatin (1761–1849) came to the attention of Jefferson by way of Madison, who described Gallatin as "sound in his principles, accurate in his calculations and indefatigable in his research." Gallatin was born in Switzerland, raised by a cousin, taught French at Harvard, was an expert on Native American culture and widowed within five months of marriage, all before settling in Philadelphia and involving himself in politics, where he most likely met Jefferson and Madison.

57. Historian James Klotter in *The Breckinridges of Kentucky* suggests that the death of John Breckinridge may have been the result of tuberculosis. This disease was prevalent at the time and later in Kentucky, with a great many of those afflicted with this bacterial lung infection dying in a matter of years or less. The disease reached epidemic proportions in the eighteenth century in North America.

58. Jefferson's support for separation of powers principles and respect among the branches of government is undeniable, but in practice, at times his position was less firm. Exemplary of this is the effort he led to repeal in part the Judiciary Act of 1801, referenced later in this book, a progressive reform that created appellate courts and eliminated Supreme Court justices from riding circuit to hear cases and later hearing appeals of their own opinions. The Federalists took advantage of this reform in the last days of the Adams presidency to put in place the so-called midnight judges, who were last-minute political appointments incoming President Jefferson despised. Overall, however, the Judiciary Act of 1801 was a forward-thinking reform.

Chapter 7

59. Thomas Jefferson to Joseph Cabell Breckinridge, Monticello, December 11, 1821, National Archives Founders Online Digital Collection.

60. Thomas Jefferson to William Clark, December 19, 1807, National Archives Founders Online Digital Collection.

61. Breckinridge Family Papers, Library of Congress, Manuscript Division, loc.gov.

62. Ibid.

Chapter 8

63. Kentucky General Assembly, Legislative Research Commission, Text of Kentucky Constitution of 1792, 1799 and 1850.

64. *Kentucky Law Journal* 73, no. 1, article 6 (1984): 206. Footnote citations omitted.

65. Ibid.; *Jefferson's Draft of a Constitution for Virginia*, May–June 1793, National Archives, Founders Online Digital Collection.

66. Jefferson's *Notes on the State of Virginia* were written in response to a request he received from a French diplomat in 1780 asking about the government, geography and history of Virginia since the diplomat was making a study of the United States. It took Jefferson years to write his notes, which are incredibly detailed and replete with maps, scientific data and his observations on the culture, laws and history of Virginia. The notes also included his views on Native Americans and enslavement.

67. "John Adams & the Massachusetts Constitution—The Declaration of Rights, 1780," Online Digital Collection of the Commonwealth of Massachusetts, mass.gov.

68. *Federalist Papers*, National Archives Online Digital Collection, 1787 and 1788.

69. The so-called British constitution is not so much a single document or codification by charter of how a nation is governed as it is a collection of the statutes, treaties, conventions and judicial decisions of the United Kingdom over time. Taken together, these laws govern how the United Kingdom operates and are referred to as the British constitution.

70. No. 47 by James Madison, *Federalist Papers*, National Archives Online Digital Collection, 1788.

71. Notably, George Nicholas in his papers, including his handwritten notes for use at Kentucky's 1792 constitutional convention, refers to Montesquieu in several places concerning relations among the branches of government. Nicholas Papers, Box 1, Folder 25, Speech in Kentucky Convention (circa 1792).

72. No. 48, *Federalist Papers*, National Archives Online Digital Collection, 1788.

73. Ibid.

74. Jefferson likewise was overseas serving as minister to France in 1787 and not at the convention in Philadelphia. Despite the limitations of time and distance, however, he sent by his own later admission "not half a dozen" letters to convention participants advocating principally for inclusion

in the document of a bill of rights securing freedom of religion, of the press, trial by jury and other rights later added to the Constitution by amendments ratified by three-fourths of the states in 1791. See Thomas Jefferson's letter to George Washington, Monticello, September 9, 1792.

75. The author can relate to the remarkable red hair of Thomas Jefferson as recorded in history, as he had the opportunity to view three samplings of Jefferson's own hair, as preserved by his daughter Martha Randolph and collected at different points in Jefferson's life. In 2012, then Librarian of Congress James Billington provided Congressman Ben Chandler (D-KY), who represented a Central Kentucky district, and me, his chief of staff, with a tour of the Library of Congress and brought out for our viewing these very hair samples. Even the hair sample from the time of his death at eighty-six visibly retained streaks of red among otherwise gray hair.

76. Maclay, *Journal of William Maclay*, 272.

77. O'Shaughnessy, *Men Who Lost America*, 84.

78. Ibid.; Hibbert, *George III*, 165.

79. Ibid.

80. In an early draft of the Declaration, Jefferson accused the king of supporting enslavement against the wishes of the public, despite the fact that Jefferson himself, as well as many in Congress, enslaved many Americans. This clause was deleted in the final text. Hibbert, *George III*, 153.

81. From Thomas Jefferson to John Adams, Monticello, March 25, 1826, National Archives Founders Online Digital Collection.

Chapter 9

82. *Autobiography of Thomas Jefferson*, 4.

83. Ibid., 160.

84. Ibid., 164.

85. *Sibert v. Garrett*, 246 S.W. 455, Court of Appeals of Kentucky, 1922.

86. Ibid.

87. *Commissioners of Sinking Fund v. George*, 47 S.W. 779, Court of Appeals of Kentucky, 1898.

88. *Sibert* at 465.

89. Ibid.

Chapter 10

90. Fleming, "Chief Justice Robert F. Stephens."
91. Jefferson had decided views of the structure and funding of public education systems on which he put a high premium. In 1779, when he was a member of the Virginia House of Delegates and shortly before becoming governor, he proposed Bill 79, "A Bill for the More General Diffusion of Knowledge," which set forth a tax-funded system of public education for up to three years for all children "male and female." Ever concerned for equality, as was Chief Justice Stephens in his *Rose* education decision in Kentucky, Jefferson said (emphasis added), "**[T]*he ultimate result of the whole scheme of education would be the teaching of all the children of the state reading, writing and common arithmetic.***"
92. *Rose v. Council for Better Education*, 790 S.W. 2d 186, Supreme Court of Kentucky !989.
93. Ibid.
94. Ibid.; foreword, in Snyder and Ireland, "Separation of Governmental Powers."
95. Chief Justice Stephens in his *LRC v. Brown* decision called on yet another founding father when he referred to a remark by President George Washington in his famous Farewell Address on September 19, 1796. This address in generally known for its provisions that the nation should avoid "entangling alliances" with foreign powers. But his prescient remark concerning the balance of power among branches of government is notable when he stated, "The spirit of encroachment of one branch of government into the functions of another tends to consolidate the powers of all the departments in one, and thus to create, whatever the form of government, a real despotism."
96. *Hayes v. State Property and Buildings Commission*, 731 S.W. 2d 797, Supreme Court of Kentucky, 1987.

Chapter 11

97. Fleming, "Budget Held Hostage."
98. *Miller v. Quertermous*, 202 SW3d 289, Supreme Court of Kentucky, 1947.
99. Ibid.
100. Memorandum to the Governor, April 2002, by the author and in his possession.

101. *Fletcher v. Commonwealth*, 163 S.W. 3rd 852, Supreme Court of Kentucky, 2005.
102. Robert Barnes, "Legal Scholars Dispute Trump's Claim to Power 'Nobody Thought the President Had,'" *Washington Post*, August 5, 2020.
103. National Archives Founders Online Digital Collection.
104. Ibid.

Chapter 12

105. Ibid.
106. As with many states, Kentucky waxed and waned over the decades with policy and legislation aimed at the right balance of crime and punishment, second chances and ways to reduce incarceration for nonviolent offenses. In 1936, Kentucky governor A.B. Chandler proposed broad-based reform in sentencing, probation and parole, much of which was passed by the General Assembly, with similar efforts being made by succeeding governors. In 2011, under Governor Steve Beshear, the legislature passed the Public Safety and Offender Accountability Act, which seems the last major reform intended to reduce incarceration for minor and drug-related offenses and invest in local resources for safe communities. In recent years, the pendulum has swung toward more legislation increasing or enhancing offender punishment in some way. For an interesting but dated history of corrections and criminal justice reform in Kentucky, see "Changing Faces, Common Walls: History of Corrections in Kentucky," U.S. Department of Justice, Office of Justice Programs Virtual Library, Kentucky Corrections Cabinet, 1988.
107. *Roper v. Simmons*, 543 U.S. 551, U.S. Supreme Court, 2005.
108. Fox Butterfield, "Inmates Go Free to Reduce Deficits," *New York Times*, December 19, 2002.

Chapter 13

109. Garrard was first elected governor by an Electoral College, succeeding Isaac Shelby in 1795. In the first ballot of a three-way race, Benjamin Logan, an ally of John Breckinridge's, received a plurality, but in a two-person run-off, Garrard defeated Logan. Although the 1799 Kentucky Constitutional Convention resulted in an amendment for the governor

to be popularly elected, Garrard was exempted from this provision and became governor again in 1799.

110. Memorandum to the Governor, April 1999, by the author and in his possession.

111. During the tenure of Governor Breathitt, the General Assembly in 1964 passed legislation to prepare a new state constitution, which was written by thirty-eight distinguished citizens in a modern-day form of a constitutional convention. Largely because of county-led opposition that feared a loss of regional power, the proposed constitution was rejected overwhelmingly by Kentucky's voters 510,099 to 140,210.

Chapter 14

112. Charles Wolfe, "Order Prohibits Sex, Gender Bias, Patton's Policy Applies to State Cabinet Workers," *Louisville Courier-Journal*, May 30, 2003.

113. Memorandum to the Governor, April 2003, by the author and in his possession.

114. National Archives Founders Online Digital Collection.

115. Those other states being Alabama, Arkansas, Indiana, Tennessee and West Virginia. Interestingly, Alaska requires a three-fourths vote to overturn the veto of appropriations and revenue bills.

116. Joe Gerth, "Bill Would Exempt Churches from Civil Rights Law," *Louisville Courier-Journal*, January 14, 2000.

117. In *Fletcher v. Office of the Attorney General ex re. Stumbo* in 2005, Justice William Cooper in his opinion for Kentucky's Supreme Court relied in part on Sections 27 and 28 to invalidate a Public Services Continuation Plan by Governor Fletcher as being an unconstitutional encroachment of the executive on the prerogative of the General Assembly as the appropriator of state funds. Cooper stated that Section 28 "has no counterpart in the United States Constitution. It is reputed to have been penned by Thomas Jefferson." In a footnote to this statement and prior to a recitation from the dissent by J. DuRelle in the 1898 *Commissioners of Sinking Fund* case where the 1792 meeting among Jefferson, Breckinridge and Nicholas is detailed, Justice Cooper states, "Judge DuRelle cited to no authority for the following account of Jefferson's role." Footnote 3 to the decision.

118. Dupre, "Political Ideas of George Nicholas," 201–2.

119. See n37, 73, supra.

120. Interestingly, less than three years before his death, in a letter to William Johnson in 1823 written from Monticello, in a comment on constitutional interpretation, Jefferson stated, "[O]n every question of construction we must carry ourselves back to the time when the Constitution was adopted, recollect the spirit manifested in the debates, and instead of trying what meaning may be squeezed out of the text, or invented against it, conform to the probable one in which it was passed." Johnson was an associate justice of the U.S. Supreme Court first appointed to the Court by Jefferson in 1804. Johnson served on the Court until his death in 1834.

Conclusion

121. National Archives Founders Online Digital Collection.

BIBLIOGRAPHY

Albert and Shirley Small Special Collections Library. Series 1: Wilson Cary Nicholas Papers, University of Virginia Library. Online repository.

The Autobiography of Thomas Jefferson. Garden City, NY: Dover Publications, 2005.

Beccaria, Cesare. *On Crimes and Punishments*. Scotts Valley, CA: On-Demand Publishing by Amazon, 2009.

Breckinridge Family Papers. Manuscript Division, Library of Congress. Online catalogue.

Cecere, Michael. *The Invasion of Virginia, 1781*. Yardley, PA: Westholme Publishing, 2017.

Dunkerly, Robert M. *The Battle of Kings Mountain: Eyewitness Accounts—The Battle That Turned the American Revolution*. Charleston, SC: The History Press, 2009.

Dupre, Huntley. "The Kentucky Gazette Reports the French Revolution." *Mississippi Valley Historical Review* 26, no. 2 (1939).

Dupre, Huntley, PhD. "The Political Ideas of George Nicholas." *Register of the Kentucky Historical Society* 39, no. 128 (July 1941).

Ellers, Fran. *Progress and Paradox: The Patton Years, 1995–2003*. Louisville, KY: Butler Books, 2003.

The Filson Historical Society, Louisville, Kentucky. Manuscripts and Photos, Online Catalogue and Research Guide.

Fleming, Denis, Jr., General Counsel to the Governor. "The Budget Held Hostage: Can the Governor Issue a Spending Plan by Executive Order:

The State's Charter Offers Guide in Troubled Times Such as These." Special to the *Louisville Courier-Journal*, June 26, 2002.

———. "Chief Justice Robert F. Stephens (1927–2002): A Legacy of Reform." Special to the *Louisville Courier-Journal*, April 14, 2002.

———. "A Proper Use of Executive Power." Special to the *Louisville Courier Journal*, April 21, 2001.

Ford, Paul Leicester, coll. and ed. *The Works of Thomas Jefferson in Twelve Volumes*. Federal ed. Washington, D.C.: Library of Congress.

Gies, Bejamin Michel. "Kentucky's First Statesman: George Nicholas and the Founding of the Commonwealth." Electronic Theses and Dissertations, Paper 2448, University of Louisville, 2016.

Hamilton, Alexander, John Jay and James Madison. *The Federalist: A Collection of Essays Written in Favor of the New Constitution, September 17, 1787*. Garden City, NY: Dover Publications, 2022.

Harrison, Lowell. *John Breckinridge: Jeffersonian Republican*. Introduction by Thomas D. Clarke. Louisville, KY: Filson Club, 1969.

———. "John Breckinridge and the Kentucky Constitution of 1799." *Register of the Kentucky Historical Society* 57, no. 3 (1959).

Harrison, Lowell, ed. *Kentucky's Governors, 1792–1995*. Lexington: University Press of Kentucky, 1995.

Heidler, David, and Jeanne Heidler. *Henry Clay: The Essential American*. New York: Random House, 2010.

Hibbert, Christopher. *George III: A Personal History*. New York: Basic Books, a Member of the Perseus Books Group, 1998.

Jefferson, Thomas. *Notes on the State of Virginia*. Annotated ed. New Haven and London: Yale University Press, 2022.

Journal of the Kentucky House of Representatives (November 8, 1798): 3–8. Legislature of Kentucky: Debates on the Kentucky Resolutions. Library of Congress online catalogue and Kentucky State University Library.

Kentucky Gazette, 1787–1840. Lexington, Kentucky Public Library. Online Digital Collection.

Kentucky General Assembly, Legislative Research Commission. Text of Kentucky Constitution of 1792, 1799 and 1850. 1965. Frankfort, Kentucky.

The Kentucky Historical Society, Frankfort, Kentucky. Online library and research tools.

Klotter, James C. *The Breckinridges in Kentucky*. Lexington: University Press of Kentucky, 2006.

Koch, Adrienne, and Harry Ammon. "The Virginia and Kentucky Resolutions: An Episode in Jefferson's and Madison's Defense of Civil Liberties." *William & Mary Quarterly* 5, no. 2 (1948): 145–76.

Legislative Research Commission. *A Citizens Guide to the Kentucky Constitution.* Research Report no. 137. Frankfort, KY: self-published, 2001.

Maclay, William. *Journal of William Maclay, Unites States Senator from Pennsylvania, 1789–1791.* Edited by Edgar S. Maclay. New York: D. Appleton and Company, 1890.

Malone, Dumas. *Jefferson and His Time.* Vol. 1, *Jefferson and the Ordeal of Liberty.* 6 vols. Boston: Little, Brown and Company. 1962.

O'Shaughnessy, Andrew Jackson. *The Men Who Lost America: British Leadership, the American Revolution and the Fate of Empire.* New Haven and London: Yale University Press, 2013.

The Papers of Thomas Jefferson, 1743–1826. National Archives, National Historical Publications and Records Commission. Online catalogue.

Patton, Paul E., with Jeffrey Suchanek. *The Coal Miner Who Became Governor.* Lexington: University Press of Kentucky, 2023.

Pearce, John Ed. *Divide and Dissent: Kentucky Politics, 1930–1963.* Lexington: University Press of Kentucky, 1987.

Reuben T. Durrett Collection of George Nicholas Papers, 1788–1890. Hanna Holborn Gray Special Collections Research Center at the University of Chicago Library, 2016. Online digital collection.

Rules of the Constitutional Society of Virginia (annotated), June 14, 1784. The National Archives Founders Online Catalogue.

Snyder, Sheryl G., and Robert Ireland. "The Separation of Governmental Powers Under the Constitution of Kentucky: A Legal and Historical Analysis of L.R.C. v. Brown." *Kentucky Law Journal* 73, no. 1 (1984).

Tauber, Gisela. "Notes on the State of Virginia: Thomas Jefferson's Unintentional Self-Portrait." *Eighteenth-Century Studies* 26, no. 4 (1993). Special issue, "Thomas Jefferson: 1743–1993: An Anniversary Collection."

Walker, Steven. *Kentucky's First Senator: The Life and Times of John Brown, 1757–1837.* Louisville, KY: Butler Books, 2024.

Wilkinson, Wallace G. *You Can't Do That, Governor!* Lexington, KY: Wallace's Publishing Company, 1995.

ABOUT THE AUTHOR

Photo credit Bruce Greenstein.

Denis Fleming Jr., a native of Louisville, received his bachelor's degree with distinction from the University of Kentucky and is a graduate of the University of Kentucky College of Law. After receiving his law degree, he practiced law throughout Kentucky with the firm Barnett & Alagia. Later, he served in Kentucky state government as general counsel to the Economic Development Cabinet under Governors Wallace Wilkinson and Brereton Jones (1988–93), general counsel to the governor and deputy secretary of the executive cabinet under Governor Paul Patton (1995–2003) and chief deputy attorney general under Attorney General Greg Stumbo (2003–4). In 2004, Fleming was appointed chief of staff to Congressman Ben Chandler (KY-6th) in Washington, D.C., with the U.S. House of Representatives. After the 2012 elections, Fleming worked with Almost Family Inc., a Kentucky-based national homecare provider as senior vice-president and legislative counsel. He resides in Washington, D.C., and Miami, enjoys travel and running and has written published book reviews. This is his first book. Fleming has one daughter, Elizabeth, who served as a policy advisor to Senate Republican leader Mitch McConnell of Kentucky. He also has two grandchildren, Esther and Amos. His brother, Ken Fleming, is a graduate of the University of Kentucky and a member of the Kentucky General Assembly in the House of Representatives.

Visit us at
www.historypress.com